What people are sa~~

Discover the essence of fatherhood in this remarkable compilation. Filled with poignant stories and thought-provoking questions, Notes from Dad *will guide you in leaving a legacy of love and understanding. Learn what truly matters and how to forge deeper connections with your children. A powerful reminder that the greatest gift we can give to another is the unshakable knowledge that they are loved.*

John David Mann and Ana Gabriel Mann, coauthors of "The Go-Giver Marriage: The 5 Secrets to Lasting Love"

The resources for moms are vast. The resources for dads are rare. Notes from Dad *offers simple and effective words of wisdom from real-world experience. Dive in. Get your hands dirty. Learn. Grow. Repeat! Enjoy this amazing compilation of solid advice from amazing dads.*

Larry Hagner is the founder of The Dad Edge Podcast and The Dad Edge Alliance Community. He is the author of The Dad's Edge **and** The Spirit of Fatherhood **among other books.**

Notes from Dad *will inspire and challenge you to become a better man and father!"*

Kent Evans, Executive Director, Manhood Journey

Notes from Dad *is an essential guide for any father striving to be his best. It's a collection of stories showcasing men who chose intentional fatherhood, demonstrating the power of presence. This isn't just an instruction manual; it's a heartfelt journey toward becoming the dad you aspire to be.*

Ryan Roy, author of Be the Dad You Wish You Had **and founder of FBI Dads (Fathers Being Involved) FBIDads.org**

Notes from Dad

**ENCOURAGING DADS AND A FATHERLESS GENERATION
WITH STORIES AND LESSONS FROM TODAY'S DADS**

COMPILED BY
JASON MEINERSHAGEN

Five Arrows Publishing

Notes from Dad
Encouraging dads and a fatherless generation with stories and lessons from today's dads
Five Arrows Publishing

Published by Five Arrows Publishing, St. Peters, MO
Copyright ©2024
All rights reserved.

No part of this publication may be reproduced, stored in a retrieval system, or transmitted in any form or by any means, electronic, mechanical, photocopying, recording, scanning, or otherwise, except as permitted under Section 107 or 108 of the 1976 United States Copyright Act, without the prior written permission of the Publisher. Requests to the Publisher for permission should be addressed to jason_ff_2005@yahoo.com, please put **Notes from Dad** in the subject line.

Limit of Liability/Disclaimer of Warranty: While the publisher and author have used their best efforts in preparing this book, they make no representations or warranties with respect to the accuracy or completeness of the contents of this book and specifically disclaim any implied warranties of merchantability or fitness for a particular purpose. No warranty may be created or extended by sales representatives or written sales materials. The advice and strategies contained herein may not be suitable for your situation. You should consult with a professional where appropriate. Neither the publisher nor author shall be liable for any loss of profit or any other commercial damages, including but not limited to special, incidental, consequential, or other damages.

All contributing authors to this anthology have submitted their chapters to an editing process, and have accepted the recommendations of the editors at their own discretion. All authors have approved their chapters prior to publication.

Cover, Interior Design, and Project Management:
  Davis Creative Publishing, DavisCreativePublishing.com

Writing Coach and Editor: Kyle Veltrop

Compilation by Jason Meinershagen

Library of Congress Cataloging-in-Publication Data
(Provided by Cassidy Cataloguing Services, Inc.).

Names: Meinershagen, Jason, compiler.
Title: Notes from dad : encouraging dads and a fatherless generation with stories and lessons from today's dads / compiled by Jason Meinershagen.
Description: St Peters, MO : Five Arrows Publishing, [2024]
Identifiers: ISBN: 979-8-9898162-0-0 (paperback) | 979-8-9898162-1-7 (ebook) | LCCN: 2024903442
Subjects: LCSH: Fatherhood--Anecdotes. | Fatherhood--Literary collections. | Father and child-- Anecdotes. | Father and child--Literary collections. | Parenting--Anecdotes. | Parenting-- Literary collections. | LCGFT: Anecdotes. | BISAC: FAMILY & RELATIONSHIPS / Parenting / Fatherhood. | FAMILY & RELATIONSHIPS / Parenting / General. | RELIGION / Christian Living / Family & Relationships.
Classification: LCC: HQ756 .N68 2024 | DDC: 306.8742/02--dc23

2024
ATTENTION CORPORATIONS, UNIVERSITIES, COLLEGES AND PROFESSIONAL ORGANIZATIONS: Quantity discounts are available on bulk purchases of this book for educational, gift purposes, or as premiums for increasing magazine subscriptions or renewals. Special books or book excerpts can also be created to fit specific needs. For information, please contact A Note from Dad, LLC, jason_ff_2005@yahoo.com

Dedication

"The influence of a mother in the lives of her children is beyond calculation." — **James E. Faust**

This book is dedicated to my mother. Karen Faye (Stanley) Meinershagen passed from this life into eternity with her Lord and Savior, Jesus Christ, on New Year's Day 2011. Affectionately known as "Granny" to us once her grandkids came along, Mom was so much more.

Mom taught me how to enjoy life and so much more — how to cook a meal, clean a house, do laundry. She prepared me for life outside of our childhood home and raised a young man whose wife would one day thank her, which gave Judy and me a goal to strive for in our own parenting.

Mom taught me how to be a self-thinker, to know what I believe and believe what I know. To fight for what's right, even if it means I'm standing alone. To stand up for the weak and defenseless. To nurture those who need love. To love the ones who do nothing to deserve our love. She showed me that it's OK to walk across the street and ask the neighbor for a couple eggs when we come up short for the recipe we're making, then to return the eggs along with a generous portion of the cake they helped make. That's something our neighborhoods need more of these days, by the way.

Mom shared with me once how much she enjoyed reading the notes I was writing to the kids on my blog, because they reminded her of her own long-lost passion for writing. Until then, I never knew where my love for writing came from, but it soon became clear that she had given up on her dream of becoming a published writer in order to raise a family.

Mom, your sacrifice did not go unnoticed. This one's for you.

In the days following her death, we found this note buried in a box among thousands of pictures. She was always taking pictures. We hated it then, but I'm grateful for it now.

Written in August 1970, three years before I was even born, my mother understood that time is a precious commodity.

TIME

Time — There is but one thing
That will not wait for you.
Time is a wonderful moment
To make your dreams come true.

Don't waste your time on foolishness
But use it on the best.
Then, when you're aged and weary
Time will bring you happiness.

Remember that time is golden
Something that does not wait.
Use it for the best of things
Do it now - Don't hesitate.

Karen Meinershagen
March 3, 1949 – January 1, 2013

Acknowledgments

"Behind every successful person is a community that inspired and encouraged him to believe in himself and to chase his dreams."
— **Jason Meinershagen**

While my writing journey started at a young age, the journey of bringing this book to fruition started in 2011 with a small handwritten note in the days following my grandmother's death. Between then and now, countless people have played a part in bringing the vision out of my mind and onto paper. Quite simply, this book would not be possible without the love, support, and encouragement of many people. If I've failed to list you by name here, please know that it was not intentional. I love each and every one of you and would not be the man and father I am today without the countless people I've come to know over my lifetime.

First and foremost, I have to acknowledge the role God has played in this project. To say I've seen God working behind the scenes for nearly two years to bring this to print is an understatement. You've shown up in places I least expect You to be, and You've stirred in the hearts of men I had never met before starting this journey in such a way that our coming together was clearly divine intervention and part of Your plan. I am nothing without the saving grace of your Son, Jesus Christ. Thank you, Lord, for the words in these pages; they were Yours before You ever placed them in the minds of each contributing author.

My wife, Judy, you've been THE most supportive and selfless person I've ever known. You've not only walked beside me through this journey of life for more than 30 years, you've made me who I am today. A selfish kid when we first met, you loved that young boy right into manhood, following me wherever I took us, for right or wrong, better or worse, through sickness and in health. I am nothing without you. I love you more than dirt, baby!

My daughter, Stephanie, there is nothing like the first child to turn a boy into a man. You woke this boy up and forced him to live for someone else instead of himself. In many ways, I grew up alongside you, learning many of the lessons of dadhood through raising you. I am blessed beyond words, and my heart melts every time I hear you scream, "*Daddy!*" and come running for your hug. Best friends!

My sons Nathan and Shane, I see me in you, and I see you in me. Being your dad has been — and continues to be — the best "job" I've ever had, the coolest "hat" I've ever worn. Watching you grow and mature into young men has been the blessing of my life. You were the inspiration to start the blog in 2011, and my "why" for writing this book. This book is for you!

My son Dan, our love for you has not changed. It never will. Your time with us was brief, but I believe God grew me by leaps and bounds in that short time. I didn't always get it right, and for my mistakes, I'm sorry, bud. Truly. My love for you has never waned over the years, and I pray for you often. I'm always here for you.

My bonus child, Cheyenne, you may officially be an adult now, but you will always be my kiddo. Thank you for being you and for bringing laughter and humor to our lives. I'm filled with joy when we're reunited, even if by the random dad jokes via text.

Dad, I don't tell you this enough, but thank you. Thank you for loving God and serving as the driving force for generational change. You did the best you could with the tools you were given, and that's all any son could ever ask or expect. The example for fatherhood and manhood that you set for your four sons is exemplary, to say the least. You showed up in ways no one knows about, and your consistency in leading and providing for

Acknowledgments

your family is what I strive for in my own fathering journey. You were my hero then, and you are my hero now. You were (and still are) the perfect dad for us. You modeled an exemplary work ethic, and you instilled in me a yearning for Christ first and family second. Thank you. I love you!

Mom, I miss you so much in moments like this. You were always my biggest fan and loudest cheerleader. Thank you for always encouraging me in my writing, even as a young boy. Your notes of encouragement in the early years of my blog before you were called home are among my most treasured memories of you. Save a place for me, and I'll see you soon! We'll sit a spell and read the last chapter first when I get there.

Jim and Jeanne (it feels weird calling you that because you both are as much Mom and Dad to me as my own parents!), from the moment I met you, I did wrong by you and your daughter. I will regret that to the end of my days. I find myself constantly working to make right by you by setting a better example for your grandsons. I am eternally grateful for the Godly example you both set to love and forgive others. You welcomed me into your family when I least deserved it, and have loved me like your own ever since. I am most grateful for allowing me the blessing of your daughter's hand in marriage. Certainly, you both played instrumental roles in who she grew to become, and I am blessed beyond words to have partnered with her in this life.

My brothers, Steve, David, and Derek, we've been close over the years, traversing many mountains and valleys along this journey. I would fall woefully short of my goal in writing this book without acknowledging the role you each have played in getting me here. There's an old expression that, *"We can pick our friends, but God picks our family."* I am blessed He picked the three of you as my brothers. I love you. I don't tell you that enough, but I do. I love you.

The many nieces and nephews in my life, you have each played a significant role in my journey. Watching you grow and become amazing people, starting your own families, has been a blessing to my soul.

My besties, Jody and Edith Read, thank you for providing me with a place of refuge and solitude to devote time for this book and the books to come. Thank you for always having my back and serving as honest sounding boards for all my crazy. Jody, you've always been my "cooler" when cooler heads need to prevail, and I'm forever grateful for you both, and that, "*It's all food.*"

My man Jamie Morgan, thank you for walking me through the trauma of my past, for holding me accountable in the intentionality of my words, for teaching me that integrity in keeping the promises we make to ourselves is just as important as integrity with others, for applying some tough love when I need it, and for encouraging me to do this. If not for you, I'd still be on autopilot, overwhelmed with where to start. You da' man!

My brother Jason Graff, I want to share this: "*A friend loves at all times, and a brother is born for a time of adversity*" (Proverbs 17:17). In my seasons of adversity, you've been there. Not just to listen to me vent, but to beat me over the head with hard doses of reality I need and to extrapolate the lesson I need in that moment. You've been instrumental in my growth as a leader, a husband, a father, a man. Thank you for challenging me when I need to be challenged, for holding me accountable when I need to be accountable, and for encouraging me to be me. Mostly, thanks for "liking" every video, even if you don't watch any of them.

My brother in Christ, Mike Gendron, I praise God for your humble service to the Lord and your desire to seek and to live within His will. I'm blessed to call you my friend and confidant. Thank you for inspiring me to evaluate my priorities in such a way that shifted my way of thinking about work, ministry, family, and our personal relationship with God. The game

Acknowledgments

changer in my life was when you showed me by example that it's OK to say "*no*" to **good** things so we can say "*yes*" to **great** things!

My F3 brothers, you are my glue! I came for the Fitness, but you hooked me with the Fellowship! Many of you contributed a chapter for this book, but so many more of you contributed to my acceleration in life. I love each and every one of you, and there's nothing you can do about it.

"Scooter," you are an amazingly beautiful, young lady whose laugh lights up the room. I've come to learn that life is too short to be taken so seriously all the time. Life is meant to be enjoyed. To live is to laugh, and you make us smile. Judy and I are blessed every moment we get to spend with you. This one's for you, kiddo!

To the men who contributed a chapter for this book, thank you! My goodness, **THANK YOU!** Thank you for believing in me and the vision for what this book can be and do as a ministry. I love each and every one of you, and I appreciate you pouring out your heart and soul. Thank you for seeing what is possible and having faith to put pen to paper! Here's to you and all that God will do through each of your lives.

"If you want to go fast, go alone. If you want to go far, go together."
— **African Proverb**

Dads are most ordinary men turned by love into heroes, adventurers, storytellers, and singers of song."
— **Pam Brown**

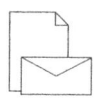

TABLE OF CONTENTS

Foreword xiii
Preface. xvii
Introduction xxi
Jason Meinershagen | Life is Short. Eat Dessert First. 1
Dave Bowen | Protect and Prepare 10
Nathan Bibb | You Choose. 16
Patrick Ritter | A Father's Resourcefulness: SUBTLE STRENGTH 22
John Burk | Some of the Best Dads Are Moms 28
Jody Read | Being a Man In a Boy's World 34
Mike Baue | I Love You a Thousand Times. 40
Bobby Christopher | A Beaming Girl-Dad. 46
Steve Koskela | A Busy Dad's Perspective 52
Jerry Krnotch | A Dad's Promise. 58
Dr. Jim Ottomeyer | Confessions of a Bad Dad 64
Joshua Davis | Attack Life With Fastballs. 70
Chad Smith | Finishing Strong 76
Henrique Friosi | Fatherhood Overcoming Challenges. 82
Willie Blue | I Survived It 88
Mike Forness | A Dad's Gift 93
Kyle Veltrop | Pain, Triumph and Joy 99
Dan Luigs | The Road Less Traveled: A Father-Daughter Journey . 105
Mike Elam | Growing My Boys! 112
Matt Crossman | Adventure-Filled Fatherhood 118
Prentice Robertson | Lessons in Servant Leadership 125
Brad Dempsey | The Power In You. 132

Jeff Erdmann | Different Perspectives 138
Matt White | The Gift of Being a Dad. 144
Mark Hollander | It's a Boy 150
Clinton Schulte | The Bigger Song and Dance Plan 155
Dan Tripp | God, Money, Beer. 161
Jaime Morgan, LPC | Painful Lessons with My Son. 167
John Whitehead | Can I Go With You?. 173
Lance Rogers | What's Your Story? 179
Bob Kolf | Only Jesus Can Save the World 185
Joel Mikos | Silent Heart: A Father's Message to His Son. 191
Tim Ruyle | Principles for a Life Fulfilled 197
Tony Schneller | Dudes, Buddies, and Best Friends 203
Afterword. 209
Conclusion. 211

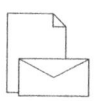

Foreword

Today, men across the country are coming together, attending seminars and training, and joining online communities, seeking to develop a healthy and clear concept of self as men and to enhance their ability to relate to their families and to others in a more insightful and positive manner.

For generations, men have paid heavily for their masculine privilege and power. They have lost touch with their emotions, health, and relationships. Today, men are examining their definition of manhood and how these definitions work in relation to fatherhood, friendships, spirituality, and community.

During my 25 years in private practice as a psychotherapist, I worked extensively with men of all ages who were struggling with mental health issues, sexual issues, and overcoming traumatic experiences. I recognized over time there seem to be four categories of recurring, unresolved issues (father/son dynamics, difficulty separating love, affection, compassion, and sex, lack of — and desire for — male friendships, and abuse). These were exacerbated by struggling and coping internally with shame, secrets, and fears.

I became fascinated with the challenges that men face, finding peace and forgiveness, addressing and resolving these issues so they can achieve healthy lives, enhance relationships, and reach their potential. This inspired me to establish the Illinois Men's Institute and Voyager Men's Experience to challenge and inspire men to mature into responsible, actively involved, caring men who could become incredible husbands, fathers, and friends.

I recently launched the Men Mentoring Men Network with the mission to empower men with the strategies, support, and tools necessary to recognize, confront, and triumph over challenges, enabling them to lead fulfilling, productive lives. We achieve this by fostering collaborative relationships, sharing experiences, and providing expertise within a network characterized by integrity, support, honesty, compassion, and a culture free of judgment. The network is comprised of three components: "Mask-ulinity – Revealing the Man Behind Workshop," "Voyager Men's Weekend" and the "Men Mentoring Men Community."

I have been married for over forty years and have one married son and two grandsons. I continue to enjoy the challenges and adventures associated with fatherhood.

In a society that often places a disproportionate emphasis on maternal roles, this anthology reminds us of the vital role fathers play in their children's lives. From the moment of conception to the milestones of adulthood, fathers serve as pillars of strength, education, spiritual guidance, and unconditional love. They are not merely spectators in the journey of parenthood but active participants, shaping the values, beliefs, and aspirations of the next generation.

In the hustle and bustle of everyday life, it is easy to overlook the significance of fatherhood. Yet, within these anecdotes lies a timeless truth: that a father's presence, no matter how subtle, shapes the narrative of his children's lives in ways both seen and unseen. Whether through laughter or tears, triumphs or challenges, the threads of paternal love weave a tapestry of strength and resilience.

In a world often swirling with discussions of gender roles, family dynamics, and societal expectations, one crucial role often stands as an

Foreword

unsung hero: fatherhood. As we navigate the complexities of modern life, it is imperative that we pause to recognize and celebrate the profound impact fathers have on shaping our communities, our families, and, most importantly, our children. This anthology, "*Notes From Dad,*" is a testament to the multifaceted nature of fatherhood and the significance it holds in our lives.

Within the pages of this book, Jason assembled fathers diverse in culture, background, and experiences, each offering their unique insights into the essence of fatherhood. From heartwarming anecdotes to thought-provoking reflections, these contributors share their journeys, challenges, triumphs, and unwavering commitment to being fathers.

Through their stories, the contributors illuminate the various facets of fatherhood: the joys of witnessing a child's first steps, the sacrifices made to provide for a family, the quiet moments of guidance and support, and the profound sense of responsibility that comes with nurturing young minds. They speak of the challenges fathers face in balancing work and family life, navigating the complexities of modern parenting, and overcoming societal stereotypes and expectations.

This anthology is not just a celebration of fatherhood; it calls upon fathers to mentor fathers and society to recognize and support fathers in their journey, to dismantle the barriers that hinder their active participation in family life, and to foster a culture that values and honors the contributions of fathers. It honors, challenges, and encourages fathers to embrace their role wholeheartedly, to lead by example, and to create a legacy of love and compassion for generations to come.

As you embark on this journey through the pages of "*Notes From Dad,*" you may be inspired by the resilience, wisdom, and unwavering dedication of the fathers whose stories grace these pages. May you, whether you are a father, a son, a daughter, or simply someone who appreciates the beauty of parenthood, find solace, inspiration, and hope in the timeless bond between fathers and their children.

Ultimately, *Notes From Dad* is more than just a book; it is a testament to the enduring power of love — a love that knows no bounds and transcends all obstacles. It is a tribute to the fathers who stand as beacons of strength, spiritual guidance, wisdom, and compassion in a world that often feels chaotic and uncertain. It is a celebration of fathers' profound impact on guiding, supporting, and shaping the lives of those they cherish, love, and hold most dear—their children.

So, to all fathers past, present, and future, I invite you to delve into these pages and rediscover the profound significance of your role in your children's lives. You are not alone; you are surrounded by men with experiences and advice willing to guide and mentor you. It simply takes five words: "Ask for what you need."

Enjoy the fatherhood journey.

Richard J. Avdoian, MS, MSW, CSP
Founder & CEO
Men Mentoring Men Networks

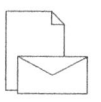

Jason Meinershagen

Preface

"How do you know what your life will be like tomorrow? Your life is like the morning fog — it's here a little while, then it's gone."
— ***James 4:14*** *(NLT)*

I hate the interstate. Always have. Always will. I've been saying it for years. I'd rather run into a burning building than work a car crash on the interstate—any day of the week. I can predict what a fire will do, where it will go, how it will act as it grows. And I can be more accurate than most meteorologists are on any given day. The interstate is another thing. A game of "chance" as cars whiz past our emergency scene at full speed. Their only care at the moment is that our big red firetruck is making them late.

As we approached the scene of a crash one afternoon, one car was against the median wall, and a motorcycle was in the middle lane of the four-lane highway. We angled the truck in such a way to block both the left and middle lanes. This provided a protected area in front of the truck to work the scene while also leaving the two lanes to our right open for traffic. Sizing up the scene, I gave my radio report and prepared to step off the fire truck onto the interstate. As I placed my hand on the door handle and began to pull, my other hand set my helmet on my head. It didn't fit. It was too small. Argh!

I immediately, instinctively, remembered ratcheting the adjustable strap so it would fit the head of my 5-year-old son. Just *five minutes* earlier, he was giggling and laughing with my helmet on his head as he played "firefighter" in the same seat while visiting the firehouse. In that flash of a moment, I recalled him standing there waving and saying, *"I love you, Daddy,"* as we pulled out of the firehouse, running lights and sirens to this car crash. I thought of him standing by the radio desk at the firehouse, eagerly listening to hear my voice on the radio.

And it was in that instant when my helmet didn't fit that I paused ever so slightly. Not long, maybe two seconds at most—just long enough to make a difference. In that brief pause, a semitruck in the lane right next to us barreled past at full speed—inches from me as I sat in my seat, pulling on the handle to open the door. At that moment, I instantly realized the blessing in that helmet and how that brief two-second pause saved my life.

Have you ever given any thought to what you would do right now if you knew with certainty that tomorrow you would die? Would you act differently? Would you treat the people around you differently? Would there be something you'd want to say to those you love? Is there something that you've put off doing that you would quickly move to the front burner? Is there something you've always wanted to do, but didn't?

What's holding you back? Are you afraid of offending someone? Are you worried you might fail? Are you afraid of embarrassing yourself? Afraid you'd be laughed at? Do you think you have more time? That your time's not up yet? That, *"It won't happen to me"*?

With reflection in the days after that incident, I was overcome with emotion at how close I really came to being killed that day. One minute, playing with my 5-year-old son who looked up to and admired me so much that he was pretending to be like me. The next minute, I was

Preface

literally inches and seconds away from being killed doing a job I loved. I was overcome with the guilt of already having missed out on so much of his and his brother's short lives so far. I questioned whether I loved the job more than my wife and kids. Such is the brevity of life. When faced with death, we often find ourselves tearing into our own life to examine our priorities.

My experience on the highway that afternoon was actually the second close call in just a few short months that should have otherwise left me seriously injured or dead, save for divine intervention and God's perfect timing. In the weeks afterward, with a fresh perspective on life, I had a clear vision for the path my life would begin to take. My purpose became obvious. I started writing notes for my children, eventually creating a blog where I would journal and leave nuggets of truth, wisdom, and advice on myriad topics. A writer by nature, it was how I knew to tell the story of my life and let my children know who I was via my own words, not someone else's, if I were to die while they're young.

I set out to chase the purpose God has placed on my heart to engage, encourage, enlarge, empower, and equip my sons to be the men God is calling them to be. In doing so, I'm pursuing my passion to do likewise for other dads, to strengthen the bond between fathers and their families as we each strive to be the husband our wives need and the dad our children deserve. That's my goal with this book.

Whether you are a son or daughter, mom or dad, husband or wife, sister or brother. Whether you grew up with a dad who was engaged and active in your life, or was absent or abusive (either physically or emotionally). Whether your dad is still alive or long removed from this life, the pages that follow contain universal and applicable wisdom for all of us, regardless of the role we fill within our family. My passion and purpose are to reach fathers and a fatherless generation. It's as simple as that.

If you're not a dad or reading this book as someone whose dad is (or was) absent in your upbringing, this book is for you, too! I believe you'll be encouraged as only their children can be when they hear their dad's and father's words speaking love and affirmation into their hearts.

If you're a father reading this book, I believe you will be encouraged that you're not alone in the struggles you face. I believe the words that follow will enlarge your heart for your family. I **know** this book will empower and equip you to be the dad you're *called* to be. The dad you *want* to be. The dad you *need* to be, for your children's sake.

The brevity of life. Life is short. You're only seconds, inches, away from the moment that will take you from your children's lives forever. Before you turn the page, I encourage you. I **implore** you. Put this book down and go enjoy them. Do a puzzle with them, Read them a book. Get on the floor and play with them. Go outside for a walk or a game of catch. Pick up the game controller and play some Fortnite (or whatever game they're playing) with them. Meet them in *their* world. On *their* level. In *their* space. On *their* time.

Go! Now!

You can come back to the rest of this book later. It'll still be here when you get back.

Close the book now, and go love on your kids.

They're worth it, and so are you.

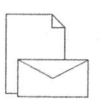

Jason Meinershagen

Introduction

"The power of a dad in a child's life is unmatched."
— **Justin Ricklefs**

There are so many lessons my dad taught me as a child. To recount them all here would take the whole book in and of itself. Even today, I'm blessed that my father is still alive and living a life worthy of the revered title, "Dad."

I remember camping with my dad as a child. We'd arrive at the site, set up camp, and spend the duration of that trip enjoying any number of things people do when they camp —hiking, fishing, swimming, roasting marshmallows, talking about life, sharing ghost stories around the campfire. Preparing to leave, we'd always go the extra mile to ensure we cleaned up our footprint. *"Leave no trace,"* I recall him saying. We'd pick up trash and debris that wasn't ours and always leave it cleaner than we found it. Still today, I find myself randomly picking up other people's trash when I'm in the park or out in public. While it might not be our responsibility to clean up after others, it *IS* our responsibility to leave it better than we found it when we got here.

In early 2011, after back-to-back incidents that should have either killed or seriously maimed me, I set out on a mission. I wanted to leave the legacy of who I was and who I am as a father to a beautiful daughter with autism, an adopted teenager, and two biological sons who were just 2 and 4 at the time, in my own words. I reasoned that if my career as a firefighter were to leave me dead or otherwise unable to be there for them as they grew, I was not content to let them know of me solely through the words of others telling them about who I was. I wanted them to hear directly from me, personally, all the things I would have otherwise been able to share with them if I were still alive. I wanted to share the wisdom of my mistakes and experiences with them and teach them the things I'd want them to know as they move through this life.

So, I started writing little notes. Nuggets of wisdom and truths I've since come to call "*Dadvice*." I probably borrowed that word from somewhere online, but I'm claiming it here because that's what this is: a collection of advice from dads. It was in 2011 that "*A Note From Dad*" was born via a small blog wherein I shared whatever rambling thoughts I felt inspired to write: no rhyme or reason. No consistency. I just wrote notes to my children when I felt compelled to write.

From the creation of that blog in 2011 to now, I've traversed many peaks and valleys to get here, to the point where you've invested your resources to read what I and other dads have to say about fatherhood. It's been quite the ride, and I'm excited to have been a part of bringing this group of men together to share their wisdom and experience. In sharing part of their story with us here, they have inspired me to be a better husband, father, brother, friend, employee, leader. and man. I hope and believe what you read here will do the same for you.

It's been my goal to finish my journey of fatherhood better than I started it, to leave my little part of the world better than I found it. I hope this book will achieve that goal in one or more of the following ways:

- **Engage** fathers in their child's world and with other dads to build a community for fathering success.

Introduction

- **Encourage** young readers to be the best version of themself and encourage other dads along their fatherhood journey.
- **Enlarge** the hearts and minds of young readers and other fathers to the world around them.
- **Empower** young readers to make healthy decisions that set their lives up for success and empower dads to be the spiritual leader of their home.
- **Equip** young readers with the knowledge, skills, and tools to be successful adults and equip fathers to lead their families with integrity and intention.

Make no mistake, the job of "*Dad*" is no easy assignment. It calls for our best, often when we're at our worst and in the hardest of times. I believe you're in the right place. I believe God has a divine plan for you through what you're about to read. Because I believe you have a desire to be the best version of yourself possible. Otherwise, you wouldn't have picked up this book. So, I invite you to turn the page with me and keep reading. Join me with some amazing men who are just normal people, dads with a desire to leave this world a little better than we found it.

> *"I could have no greater joy than to hear that my children are following the truth."*
> — **3 John 1:4** (NLT)

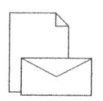

Jason Meinershagen

Life is Short. Eat Dessert First.

"At the end of your life, you will never regret not having passed one more test, not winning one more verdict, or not closing one more deal. You will regret time not spent with a husband, a friend, a child, or a parent."
— **Barbara Bush**

It was shortly before 7:00 a.m. on an otherwise normal day in the middle of the week. I had just put my fire gear on the truck to "check in" for my 48-hour shift when the tones dropped — an apartment fire! This one was close, just a couple blocks behind the firehouse. We were there in less than two minutes.

As we arrived, smoke was venting through the second-floor window, and neighbors reported that the occupant was nowhere to be found, so she might still be inside. Jumping off the truck, I walked around the rear of the building. As the company officer, it was my job to circle the building to get a 360-degree view of the building, looking for fire, persons trapped, points of entry, egress, and more.

Finishing that before my firefighter had the hose line at the front door, I stepped inside and called out, *"Fire department! Can you hear me?"* The second time I called out, I heard a faint moan from the back of the apartment. The first floor was covered in trash and debris, discarded fast-food bags, empty beer boxes, and wine bottles. With fire raging on the second floor above me, I pushed my way through the nearly knee-high pile of trash down the hallway toward the direction I heard the moan, continuing to call out, "*Fire department!*"

Rounding the corner to the living room, I found her. Slumped over the couch in a semiconscious state, she looked at me with dazed eyes and mumbled out a slurred, "*What do you want?*"

"*Your house is on fire; we gotta get you out of here!*"

She scoffed at me with a moan of disgust that said all I really needed to know. She was out of it.

"*Can you stand and walk?*"

Looking around and seeing no signs that her apartment was on fire (sans the fully dressed firefighter in her living room at 7:00 a.m.), she mumbled, "*Ain't no fire, and I ain't going nowhere!*"

I tossed the coffee table that was littered with half-empty soda cups out of my way and reached down to pick her up. Resisting my attempts to grab her for a moment, she finally conceded and went limp. I put my arms under hers, wrapped her arms around my neck, and dragged her backward down the hall, back through the mess of trash toward the front door. I met my firefighter just inside the front door, and we handed her off to police officers on the front porch who would carry her to waiting paramedics for treatment.

Isn't that indicative of life for many of us? The house is burning around us, and we don't even know it and don't want to get off the couch. Life is happening right outside the front door, and we're stuck on autopilot. We're so comfortable in our comfort that we don't want to risk being uncomfortable, even when we know there is a better life right through that next door. We just have to acknowledge that there's a problem going on right above us, all around us. We have to acknowledge that the, "*House is on fire, and we gotta get moving!*"

A career in the fire service spanning three decades brings more moments of clarity about life's priorities than I can ever begin to recount. I have five "Life Saving" awards in a box somewhere in my basement, a scratch on the surface of how many times I've been a part of bringing someone back to life, and not even a blip for the number of people we couldn't bring back. For this save, I have a piece of medal in the same dusty box at the bottom of my closet, a piece of medal to remind me that some people don't want to be saved.

Seeing death up close and personal reminds us of the brevity of life. It awakens our minds to our own immortality and offers us an opportunity to see life through a different lens, a fresh perspective on our journey through this life. Being a witness to death often jolts us from our slumber back into a reality that sees us redefining our priorities to ensure we're living life to the fullest. For many, it calls us into a conversation with our Creator about where we're going and why.

My mom read thousands of mystery and romance novels in her lifetime, and she would always read the last chapter first. She explained to me once that she did that because she wanted to know how it ended so she could read the rest of the book with the ending in mind. It helped her understand the characters and their role within the story as it developed so she could better see how it all came together in the end. I never fully understood why, until she was gone.

If we could live this life knowing how it ended, how much easier would it be? How cool would it be to know how it all comes together in the end? Would we live differently? Would we treat people differently? Would we act differently? Would we love deeper? Trust more? Seek less to be understood and try harder to understand? Forgive more easily? Laugh louder? Work less and play more? Enjoy the simple things with more passion?

Here's the thing: We **DO** know how it ends! Five minutes after we die, we'll be in front of God, accounting for this life on Earth, answering for all that we've done and not done with the time He gave us here.

I was raised in a Christian home. We were in church every Sunday morning, back on Sunday nights, and again on Wednesday nights for more. The foundation my parents provided for me was rooted in a belief in God as our Creator and a faith in Jesus Christ as our Savior. Once I turned 18 and went to college, I turned my back on God and church. I took a warped version of scripture and adopted the mantra, "Once saved, always saved." I reasoned that I can live this life however I want and still make it to heaven. I grew further and further away from God, and life seemed to support that belief. For a while.

In the months after the attacks of September 11, 2001, and in the face of having become a dad earlier that year, I began wrestling with what life in eternity would look like. I recall telling my wife, *"I don't want to stand before God when I die and have Him say to me, 'Jason, you turned your back on me for a while. But you placed your trust in me once, so yes, you are welcome into heaven. But your children, I don't know them, so they can't come. I don't know them because you didn't introduce them to me.'"* I adamantly believed I didn't want that on my conscience for all of eternity, that the eternal damnation of my children was because I didn't introduce them to the God who created them.

I still feel that today. Teenagers, now, as I write this, you're coming into your own understanding of faith, God, who Jesus is, and who you are in relation to the rest of creation and our Creator. I see you questioning the church as we've known it for your lifetime up to now. It's good that you're questioning these things. It truly is, bud. It means you're seeking to find yourself and your place in this world.

My faith and belief in Jesus Christ as Lord and Savior cannot extend to you. It's the one thing I cannot pass on to you. I can share Jesus with you, and I hope I have done that well. I can talk about my love for Christ and all He has done for me, and I hope I have done that enough. I can read scripture and tell you all the Bible stories, though I know I've failed miserably here. I can live this life to glorify God (I know I've fallen short many times in many situations), but I cannot put that belief into you. It's called "free will" for a reason. It's your right to accept or deny the free gift of Christ.

Being called "Dad" is my greatest honor in this life. I've not always lived this out, but please know that there is no other role I fill that is more rewarding or more important to me than being your dad. When I started on this journey of fatherhood, I had high intentions and higher hopes to do much better than I have so far. For all the times I've failed you or let you down, I am so very sorry. I have a lot of regrets in this life. Coming up short as the dad you desire and deserve is my greatest.

What do I want for you? Simple. I want to see you in heaven. As you navigate this life, I want three things for you. Just three:

1. **BE YOU**

   Of all the people who ever walked this planet or ever will, you are the only *you*. Tens of BILLIONS of people have lived throughout history, and there are no copies. I'm blessed beyond words that God chose me to be your dad. To know He knew you infinitely for all of time, even before He formed you in your momma's womb, is astounding. To know He chose me to raise you and prepare you for this life is overwhelming and humbling. Just be you, bud. In your uniqueness, God has a purpose for you in this life. I believe that with all my heart and with every fiber of my being. He created you to do something in this life, to bring Him glory through your life. The angels in heaven celebrated when you were born, and they shouted for joy when you professed your belief in Him. Be you.

Don't ever apologize for it, and don't ever try to hide the real you. You're amazing, not for what you have done or will do with your life but for **WHO YOU ARE**! Don't ever let anyone tell you otherwise.

2. CHASE YOUR DREAMS

I don't care who you become or what you do for a living. Do you want to be an astronaut? I want that for you! Do you want to drive a street sweeper? I want that for you! Do you want to own your own business or be a YouTube star? Sweet! I want that for you! Whether you want to sell million-dollar homes or be the guy who cleans and preps the houses for sale, I want that for you! You want to stay single or get married, have kids or not have kids, I want that for you. I mean, full disclosure, I have dreams for all those things, but they're MY dreams not yours. What I want is for you to become who YOU want to be. I want you to relentlessly and unapologetically chase YOUR dreams. I'll love you regardless. I'll be proud to call you my child, no matter what. Because I *do* love you, and I *am* proud of you! Grandkids *would* be nice, though —just saying. :)

3. KNOW GOD

I refuse to stand before God when I die and have it said that I never introduced you to Him, that I failed in my duty to live out Christ's commission. God gives us the right to choose for ourselves whether to believe and accept Him or deny Him, so I cannot choose that path for you. But I *can* put the path in front of you so you can make your choice. Scripture tells us, *"All have sinned and fall short of God's glory"* (Romans 3:23). It also tells us that although we deserve death, *"The free gift of God is eternal life in Christ Jesus"* (Romans 6:23). Someone stepped in and willingly accepted that death for you, though. That "someone" is Jesus. *"Christ died for our sins according to the Scriptures, was buried, and was raised on the third day"* (1 Corinthians 15:3-4).

To know God is my utmost desire for you, that YOU know and trust in the God of creation and place your trust and faith in his Son, Jesus Christ. This place is not our home. We are temporary residents of this physical life, and when we pass from this physical life, we will live for eternity in one of two places. Our final destination for eternity is our choice and our choice alone. Whether you and I will be reunited in eternity is your choice. I want nothing more from this life than to know you in the next one.

I've seen death up close and personal more times than I could ever recount. I've forgotten more of the ugly side of my job as a firefighter than I'll ever remember. In hindsight, maybe that's a good thing. What I take away from all that is the title of this chapter and my mantra for how to live life (though I still have some work to do on myself in this arena):

Life is short. Eat dessert first.

Enjoy your time here because how long you're in this game of life isn't up to you. It's completely up to the Coach when He pulls you out. You don't get a say in that timeline.

So, take that sick day now and then, even if you're not sick. Don't wait for the weekend to go fishing; go in the middle of the week. Watch the clouds fly by for hours on end or the birds and squirrels in the backyard. Eat lunch with your kid at school. Better yet, sign him out and go someplace together for the day. Let him choose where. Sign up for that 5K. Write that book you've been putting off. Ask the girl out. Take the leap. Start that business you've been dreaming about. Trust your gut. Love deeply. Forgive easily. Never pass up an opportunity to tell the people in your circle that you love them. Love is a good thing. It's what connects us and drives us to be a better version of ourselves.

Most important, live your life to glorify God. He doesn't promise it will be easy when you do, but He does promise to be with you. Seek His will for your life, and He will reveal it to you. When you don't think God is revealing His will to you, remember He already has: *"He has shown you what is good. And what does the Lord require of you? To act justly and to love mercy and to walk humbly with your God"* (Micah 6:8).

The house is burning right above you. You're on the couch, and someone just walked in your front door to save you. Don't wait until it's too late to make the one decision that will live with you for the rest of this life…and the next. Get off the couch and live! You're worth it.

> *"If I could give you only one thing in this life, I would give you the ability to see yourself through my eyes. Only then would you begin to realize how truly special and amazing you are … to me and to the world. Believe in yourself."* — **Unknown**

Jason Meinershagen | Life is Short. Eat Dessert First.

A father to five beautiful children, Jason has been married to the same amazing woman for more than 30 years. He and Judy have been — and continue to be — active in their community, serving and volunteering in various roles within a multitude of ministries and charitable organizations that support and care for children and their families.

After years of trauma endured as a firefighter for more than three decades, Jason has come to understand what it is to endure pain and an ever-present pressure to perform. This journey through post-traumatic stress has fueled a fire within him to advocate for mental health services and support within the first responder community. Fueled by a burning passion for changing his life's outcome, He has found that his past and his pain have met with his passion at a crossroads,.

Jason is passionately on mission to fulfill his purpose and leave a legacy of strengthening family relationships. This passion has led him to engage, encourage, and empower dads to fulfill their God-given role as the leaders of their families by equipping them to be active and engaged in the lives of their families.

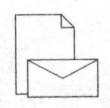

Dave Bowen

Protect and Prepare

"... do not forget my teaching, take to heart my commands;
For many days, and years of life, and peace, will they bring you."
— **Proverbs 3:1-2**

As children, we expect our parents to protect us through childhood and prepare us for success as adults.

As parents, we set out with the intent to teach our children well so they may find peace in their lives and have it better than we did. Our intent is to protect our children until they can fend for themselves and to prepare them by equipping them with tools to navigate this ever-changing world.

As children, we should expect our parents to protect us through childhood and prepare us for success as adults. That does not seem like too much to ask. It is here where experience often does not match intent. We are flawed as humans, and the world is filled with complexity that creates many varied reactions.

"I will never do that to my children! I will not force them to go through this!"

As sons and daughters, we can make emotional declarations rising out of painful childhood experiences. Childhood traumas can make an indelible mark on our development. Some are simple reactions to the lessons and pains of growing up. Some people experience significant traumas and abuses. We react and create a resolve that hopefully launches a pendulum effect where painful experiences skip the next generation. We intend as parents to ensure our children have it better than we did. We want to deliver expectations to be protected through childhood and prepared for success as an adult.

Speaking from experience, I had made such a declaration of my intent for when I would become a dad. I was reacting to my own childhood experience. My sister and I learned from a dad of great character. He was a great leader who influenced many people and created a significant impact on quite a few lives. He had his flaws, as all humans do. He became a parent when he was barely an adult himself, at the age of 21. He struggled to reconcile the challenges of this world, and the stress of his work, serving as a police officer, took its toll. These elements contributed to a marriage that ended in divorce after 12 years.

Now, this is not that traumatic compared with many childhood experiences. In fact, our childhood was rather good. My dad remarried, and we have a younger brother and sister who witnessed a strong example of marriage up until my dad's sudden death at 64. He was a man of great character with a big heart, who developed others into great leaders. His influence and impact on others were noted at his funeral by the large turnout to pay their respects and share how my dad had impacted their lives. He lived with the intent to protect others as a police officer and prepare his kids with life lessons for success in adult life. I relay this note from Dad, noting that life is messy, and offer it as an example where the expectation is to protect and prepare our children with positive intent. However, delivering on that expectation is where many dads fall short of perfection.

Today's world continues to change at a rapid pace. We have access to unlimited information and entertainment. The amount of information available to us would double every 100 years until 1900. By the middle of the 20th century, it would double every 25 years. Now, it doubles every year, and the time information takes to double continues to increase in speed. This pace makes life messy and creates all kinds of reactions. The pace of life, complexity of information, and infinite possibilities available to us leave little time for wonder and reflection. If we are to protect and prepare our children for the future, it requires time to reflect on the rapid pace of change so we may put it in proper perspective. This pace of change makes it even more challenging to understand how to protect our children, let alone prepare them for the future.

It is commonly understood that we pass on personality traits from generation to generation. There are many good traits, and some are not so good. Although my vow for when I became a dad was made with the best intentions, pulling it off is another story. I was keenly aware of my own tendencies when reacting to the pressures of the world. I worked to ensure I learned how to navigate life's challenges with intentional responses instead of emotional reactions. I worked at my marriage, which is heading toward 32 years of success. I had good intent in making that vow: "I will never do that to my children! I will not force them to go through this!" I intended to protect and prepare my kids. Although I have succeeded in many ways, I had failures as well. After all, I am human with my own messiness and blind spots. Some of those blind spots have had unintended impacts on my son and daughter.

I realize now, later in life, that part of my reaction to childhood was to go it alone. I was determined not to depend on others so I would not be let down or relive painful experiences. The intent was to protect myself from pain; however, going it alone is contradictory to the Catholic faith that I openly embraced and entered into as an adult. When going it alone, the road to success is longer and much more difficult. The road is longer and much more difficult. As a Christian, when you surrender your pride, let go and let God help prepare your path, it is then that you find peace. It is difficult, and surrendering to God's will for your life requires courage. I was not taking enough time to listen, reflect on experiences, and adjust to better protect and prepare my children for success. I continue to learn and work at this because it is a lifelong process of growth and continuous learning. This note from Dad asks that you listen, let go, and learn to hear God's intent for your life. It is not just Mom and Dad who can prepare and protect you through your life.

As a parent, I had intended to set lofty standards and create worthy goals for my kids to achieve. This is also a reaction to protect from childhood experiences and pain. In some ways, I communicated the need to be perfect while not allowing enough room for failure, learning, and growth. I intended to prepare for success while executing with some blind spots. In hindsight, I could have been more patient to allow more space and grace to learn and grow. There is a paradox when it comes to protecting your children. You must allow them enough space to explore and fail independently, even learning some painful lessons. It is challenging as a dad to step back and allow painful things to happen to our children. There is nothing quite like the love of a father for his children. God continually invites us to follow Him.

"The Father loves the son and has given everything over to him."
— **John 3:35**

Look beyond the execution and peek into the heart of your dad's intent to see the love and desire to protect you from painful experiences while preparing you for success.

We are on this journey, seeking to align our heads, hearts, and habits so we may live with courage and find peace. Our parents seek to protect us during childhood and prepare us for success as adults. What is your estimated arrival time for achieving God's goals for your life? We are asked to elevate our thinking, transform our hearts, and commit to living in alignment with God's intent for our lives. Are we prepared to let go of past experiences and live in the present? Are we prepared to walk forward with hope? We may strive for perfection; however, we are called to understand that we must allow for space and grace to fall short, learn, and grow in this life to improve continuously.

We are created perfectly imperfect. We must embrace our imperfections with humility, surrender our pride, and look toward God's intent for good to come from all experiences. It is God's way as our heavenly father to protect us and prepare us for the next life.

> *"Trust in the Lord with all your heart, on your own intelligence do not rely; In all your ways, be mindful of him, and he will make straight your paths."* — **Proverbs 3:5-6**

I relay this by asking to focus on intent and the good life lessons while learning from negative experiences on which you do not want to pass. This note from Dad asks for adult children to look beyond the human faults that all dads have and see the intent to protect and prepare while embracing your personal legacy of good family traits. May you embrace your family legacy, as it is your story. Like it or not, the choice is up to you to reframe your story and create the meaning and significance of your journey. May you look past the faults and failures to note the intent, find the wisdom in your dad's life lessons, and vow to live your life protecting and preparing your own children, passing on a legacy one level better than your own experience.

Dave Bowen | Protect and Prepare

Dave serves as director of leadership development at Hogan Transportation Companies. He is also the principal and founder of True North 2 Success, a coaching and consulting firm that transforms spirit-driven leaders professionally and personally so that they can achieve their potential.

He is curious to learn about others and understands that everyone has a divine uniqueness and perspective to contribute. Leaders like working with Dave, stating they are challenged to grow at the edge of their comfort zones.

With more than 35 years of executive operations leadership and coaching experience, few things are more rewarding to Dave than helping people transform by providing leadership guidance and training to elevate their awareness, transform their habits, and achieve performance levels even they did not believe possible.

Dave has been married for 32 years, has two adult children, and enjoys spending time with family, serving at his parish, hiking, golfing, and reading to learn and grow continuously.

Nathan Bibb

You Choose

The most important life lesson was staring me in my face my whole life, and I didn't learn it until nearly a year after my dad's passing.

Growing up and attending the international studies magnet schools in the St. Louis public school system exposes you quickly to significant differences in the world at an early age. With classmates from around the globe, there were many of us who fell into the "minority" category. Elementary school was safe and normal enough, but that wasn't the case through middle school and into high school. Bunche Middle was located on the edge of The Ville, one of St. Louis' most violent neighborhoods. Gunshots weren't uncommon and even occurred on the school's campus twice in my three years of attending. With a large number of Bosnian refugees coming to St. Louis and the international studies program being a good fit for them, middle school became a powder keg for what was to come in high school.

Born and raised in St. Louis city, I saw a lot of people who felt victimized by their environment. Attending high school in north St. Louis and being a freshman during the 1999 Soldan race riot, while at the same time playing hockey for one of the most expensive schools in the greater St. Louis area, I grew up with exposure to a wide range of life. It would have been easy to compare my middle-class upbringing to my teammates and be discouraged. It wasn't until much later in life that I realized a mindset that I had been unknowingly living by. There are a lot of things in life that we can't control, but you must understand that YOU CHOOSE. I chose to look at my Priory teammates as what I could achieve. I chased that lifestyle rather than feeling like it must not be for me because it was so different than the environment I saw in the city.

As a kid growing up, the toughest years were during middle school. Transitioning to a new school and all of the peer pressures of adolescence was a turning point for many of my friends and me. I could keep my head down, work, and get through. Or act up to be more included as one of the "cool kids" and set my life on a different trajectory. I'm thankful for both my mom and dad, who worked hard and sacrificed, instilling work ethic and pride in me. When I was young, especially in these middle school days, I felt invincible. But while I wasn't afraid of much, I was always fearful of disappointing my parents.

I attended the University of Missouri-Rolla, and it had a "small" campus feel that contributed to my success. The small town didn't have a whole lot going on during the week, making it easier to focus on academics during the school week. It helped me to learn the benefits of not procrastinating. I spent my college and the early years thereafter hyper-focused on my career. Shortly after moving back to St. Louis in 2008, I met the love of my life, Whitney. Because she worked nights and Saturdays, it became easy for me to put in an excessive number of hours at work.

Fast forward to 2017, my life was changing in a way I didn't expect. In preparation for Whitney and my firstborn. I began making a concentrated effort to work a more reasonable number of hours. For a few weeks, my dad kept mentioning we needed to get together, which was pretty out of character for him. On February 12, I was playing for the ManAdvantage team in a hockey tournament supporting autism in Shaw Park when my dad and I were finally able to talk in person. It was at this moment that I found out my dad had been diagnosed with Stage-4 pancreatic cancer. I was devastated. I didn't know what to say. I apologized to him, and we held each other tight. During our ride back to my house to have lunch with Whitney, we listened to Lukas Graham's "Funeral", a song that I'd just been introduced to that week.

My dad's fights through chemotherapy were a rollercoaster. The cancer had already weakened his body to the point where he didn't have much strength to recover from the treatments, which led to hospitalization after hospitalization. In March, he had a portion of his bowel die, which leaked toxins into his body and caused him to become septic; he was lucky to survive it. He kept fighting, and my mom kept supporting. He made it seem like he wasn't in pain, and she made it seem effortless. Despite a colonoscopy bag, valves for draining his lungs, and a chemo port, he continued to fight hard. With my busy work schedule, I made sure I visited him at least once a week.

My fondest memory was on May 11 when we went on a random outing. Somehow, he had more energy than he had in weeks, and he was on a mission to stop by a number of stores. We went to Whole Foods, and he bought the most expensive caviar he could find. Then we went to a number of other stores for random things he felt my mom needed. I remember driving home that night, realizing the extent to which the cancer had physically deteriorated him. It was the first time it had hit me that the end could be near.

My cutting back on work hours became focused time to spend with my dad. Exhausted from the week, a number of my visits with him became me falling asleep on the couch while spending time with him. At his last hospital visit before being put on hospice, my dad confided in me that even those times that I'd fallen asleep, he cherished the "extra" time we spent together. I did, too. Somehow, even while sleeping, I could feel his presence.

His last weeks were challenging; he was in a lot of pain. His decline led to his oncologist taking him off of chemo. I encouraged meeting with one of my friends, with whom he was familiar, to discuss palliative care, as she works in the hospice industry. I knew my dad wanted to make it to meet my firstborn in person, but that date was nine-plus weeks out. Slowly, I saw he was finally allowing himself to stop the fight.

On June 13, 2017, at 12:30 a.m. while listening to Disc 2 of Pink Floyd's "The Wall," my dad took his last breath right after I'd returned to the room from putting away his caviar that we'd all just sampled. With my hand on his arm, surrounded by my mom and all of his kids, my dad was gone. Whitney, pregnant with our first child, Mackenzie, was due to be born around my birthday in August. But due to complications with a sudden onset of preeclampsia, Mackenzie arrived nearly eight weeks early at 11:12 p.m. on June 22, 2017. Just nine days after my dad took his final breaths. At that moment, I wrote these details down and saved them on my phone. To this day, I repeatedly read them to desperately hold on to those final moments and the wide range of emotion I experienced at that time.

June was a rough month. I'd lost my dad, and for the first time had others calling me dad. Separation anxiety was high. I have blamed myself for my dad not having the opportunity to meet Mackenzie. It would be easy for that weight to hold me back. I found it hard to concentrate and felt a lot of depression when not spending time with Mackenzie. It would have been easy to shut down. A few months went by and, mentally, I began feeling stronger. Rather than slow down, I felt an urge to push forward. My dad always told me I would become a lawyer or a politician; I didn't think I'd do either. Things fell into place, and it was impossible not to see the opportunity that led me to run for public office and eventually be elected in April 2019.

I still have to continually make a conscious effort to CHOOSE a positive reaction to these events. To this day, I have separation anxiety when I've missed my kids after back-to-back nights of meetings keeps me from them. I know, however, that the sacrifices I'm making now are to ensure a bigger and brighter future for my daughters, Whitney, and my community when I am no longer here.

A time will come when I, too, will not be here for my family and friends. More than anything in the world, I want my daughters to know how much their dad loved them and that I want them to CHOOSE. Choose to use my passing as a motivator for them to continue working hard and fight to make a positive difference in their lives, their friends, and their community. May they carry this compilation with them through life and find value from each contributor that helps them navigate the world without me.

Through different seasons of life, you'll face challenges from peer pressure, work commitments, stress at home, and the ever-changing world. It is absolutely critical to stay conscious that YOU have the option to CHOOSE.

Nathan Bibb | You Choose

Nathan Bibb was born and raised in south St. Louis city. He graduated high school from St. Louis public schools while playing ice hockey for some of West County's most affluent teams. Growing up immersed in diverse cultures helped shape Nathan's perspective on life and his drive to achieve and serve. Starting with serving in the construction industry, in 2017, life changes propelled Nathan onto a path that only his father had ever suspected. Nathan's "why" are his two daughters, Mackenzie Rae and Bailey Scott, named after both of their grandfathers. Their happiness and security are his guiding light.

Patrick Ritter

A Father's Resourcefulness: SUBTLE STRENGTH

It was a cold but sunny winter morning in the early 1990s in St. Louis. I was riding with my dad through the city in his truck. We had just wrapped up a job moving furniture for the friend of a relative at their city home. I was not a motivated helper that morning, but Dad needed an extra hand.

The rest I found on that sun-warmed vinyl bench seat ended abruptly when the truck suddenly died on the highway. Smoke was billowing from under the hood as he turned on the hazard lights, and we began to slow to a roll. Dad switched lanes to the shoulder of the highway and looked under the hood. I don't remember exactly, but in a few minutes, he assessed the problem and said something like, "It's overheated; looks like the heater core is out, and we got the intake manifold gasket out."

Before the days of cell phones, I figured we'd have to walk to the nearest parts store. Dad would then be under the car, fixing the problem with cars whizzing by on the highway. Towing a car to the shop or using roadside assistance weren't options for him. He'd work on it until it was done, regardless of the weather, and he did this so many times growing up.

What made this fix; it was very short and very cheap. In about 30 minutes, his solution came from his truck and some trash by the side of the road.

- The neck of an old metal gas can in the truck bed was cut and used to connect the intake and output hoses from the heater core.
- The gasket was replaced using a discarded milk carton cut with an X-Acto knife in the shape to match the old one, now crumbled under the water neck that sat atop the intake manifold.
- An old milk jug kept in the cab with some yellowish water was used to refill the radiator.
- He drove us home after a quick stop by the parts store to get the real parts for the real job to be done later at home.
- As a friend told me when I shared this story, "That's some straight-up MacGyver stuff!"

Beyond the resourcefulness and problem-solving he demonstrated, it was his almost ever-present calm demeanor that I remember about that day. The subtle strength shown in this situation is needed from us all at times, but this is especially the case for fathers. While resourcefulness alone is becoming a lost art in our technology-driven modern times, the bigger takeaway from the experience was how you handle yourself as a man.

My dad has never been one for the spotlight or recognition. He has, however, been a vital cog in many wheels. He served in the Army and then worked as a mechanic, problem-solving tractors and lawnmowers, and eventually, he was building fighter aircraft. Dad has been an active contributor to parish priorities, coached kids' sports teams, and, most vitally, as an engaged dad and grandfather raising quality people. While he's never been the leader of many by title or made decisions from the C-suite with a significant position or rank, he has undoubtedly been a leader for decades.

Dad made the parish picnic signs with stencils and spray paint. He carved countless crosses from wood that became First Communion gifts for many families and friends. He brought new life to countless bikes and lawnmowers for us that came from the trash. For years, he sold coffee at work for 25 cents a cup and paid for various odds and ends at home. He gave away so many hours of free car, mower, tractor, and home improvement skilled labor for so many.

Buying old vehicles, like his Sierra for very little and keeping them running for a few, maybe five years, was what he did. He loved that truck because it was good on gas, and with an inline six-cylinder engine, there was enough room for a damn lawn chair in the engine bay so he could work on it in comfort. This was one of his many ways to save money. With five kids in private school, being frugal was essential growing up. While I learned the importance of living simply from my parents, Dad got the masterclass from his.

As number six of 13 siblings growing up in a two-bedroom home, being considerate of and adjusting to the needs and wants of others was how he was built. Servant leadership was probably not said, but the family lived it out daily. Bartering or donating favors for friends, family, and parishioners was a means of subsistence growing up and a continued responsibility as an adult.

My parents, especially Dad's ability to strategically work overtime, made so much possible for our family. Dad would work seven-day weeks and, for many years, on the third shift. He'd ask his coworkers if they "really wanted" to work their Saturday and Sunday shifts so he could cover them instead. He rarely got a good night's sleep for 20 or more years of his career. Then, he'd work at home in the morning on the many favors others needed from him, likely exhausted but still maintaining that trademark patience. It's a strength far fewer people, including myself, identify with today.

What follows are not his words but instead principles I learned from his examples:

1. You don't need a high-profile personality to influence and lead others.

    - Subtle strength possessed by a highly skilled yet humble contributor can be a megaphone all its own. This can be the case in your church, your community, or your company, where many jockey for attention or position. When you're good or great at something, people will figure it out. You don't even have to tell them. What's critical is doing your best while demonstrating humility, kindness, and genuine care for others.

    - Being widely followed is not the only way to create a "personal brand." People will know the quality person you are through your interactions with them, far more than anything shared online.

2. You do need to be known for the character fundamentals.

    - Being present and showing up means more than you know, not just for people who can do something for you, but also for those most in need of someone to listen and understand them. Don't learn the many ways to politely end conversations. You may be the only person who they can share with.

    - There is no faster way to communicate to someone that they are unimportant than by being late. You can always call to let them know you're on the way, but even when volunteering or doing favors, treat it like work.

    - You know what you know, but don't risk harming yourself or others figuring some things out. It's OK to concede that you don't know how to do something, and when necessary, ask for help or pay a professional.

3. Strive for an "others-first" mindset. Be a servant leader.

    - "Not needing anyone" is a sure path to an empty existence.

- If you don't believe in something greater than yourself, you lack purpose, like a rudderless ship. Having faith means you're accountable for yourself and others, too. You are striving for rewards greater than your own personal satisfaction.
- Service builds character. Never forget to give back and care for those in your family and community. You should do it anytime you see a need, and you are able to help. You also never know if or when you will need someone's help in return, so withhold your judgments.

4. Strength is not what the world would have you think it is.
   - Strength is also durability. It's not just about cardiovascular endurance or bench presses.
   - The celebrated John Wayne cowboy and Jack Reacher Hollywood badass characters solving problems with violence, leading solitary lives, womanizing, or drowning their problems in alcohol with no accountability to a family or community are no heroes.
   - Life will continually knock you down. It will require you to persevere. You will want to quit things; give up on people; and take the easiest, shortest path, but don't. Many are relying on you, and being a consistent, present, and caring figure for decades takes a strength few appreciate.

These points don't answer everything you need to know in life as a fatherless child, or if you are a dad figuring things out for yourself. They are, however, a start. The next time you don't see yourself as a leader, or that you're not affecting lives, remember that being the most visible or celebrated by many is not the only way to measure impact. If you live a good life that gets modeled by even just a handful of people who love you, then pour that same or greater goodness into the world. It creates an impact for generations! Subtle can absolutely be strong.

Patrick Ritter | A Father's Resourcefulness: Subtle Strength

Patrick is a single dad raising two teenage boys in the St. Louis area. He has many interests and pursuits, including the following.

- As a corporate trainer, Patrick is passionate about helping insurance agents learn and develop product subject-matter expertise.
- Patrick provides comprehensive financial planning and investment management with no product sales or commissions through Core Planning for high-earning professional clients.
- He writes a fly-fishing blog for anglers passionate in their pursuit of variety.
- Patrick also loves to connect with the outdoors through photography and involvement in F3, an organization that stands for Fitness, Fellowship, and Faith. He has been a leader in F3 and leads service projects for his church.

This project is an opportunity to share more about the man who has done so much for me. Patrick has learned for the many who weren't fortunate enough to have a dad like his in their life.

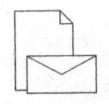

John Burk

Some of the Best Dads Are Moms

I was immediately intrigued when asked if I was interested in contributing a chapter for this project. What are the "nuggets of wisdom" I want to pass down to my children? What insights might be interesting for others? As I considered it, it became clear I might have a different perspective to share. The best insights I have on being a dad are things I learned from my mother and daughters. Let me explain.

I was born in 1968 and came along later in my parents' life. My dad and mom were born in 1925 and 1926, respectively. They were children of the Great Depression, and Dad served on a destroyer in World War II. They were part of the so-called Greatest Generation, and had very specific ideas about life. They saved money. Nothing went to waste. They believed in family time and going to church. These beliefs guided them.

I have been saying *they*. I should have been saying *she*. Dad died from lung cancer when I was 5. I presume I would have gotten the same lessons from both parents, but God had other ideas. I have an older sister, but she is 18 years my senior. She was grown, married, and lived out of state for my youth. It was just Mom and me, so she was my example of what to be as a parent. Luckily she is the strongest person I have ever known. As I look back with admiration at what Mom did, these are the most important lessons I want to teach my children:

WORK ETHIC AND PERSISTENCE. Mom was a stereotypical 1950s/1960s housewife. She had not worked outside the home for 24 years prior to Dad dying. They were frugal, but there wasn't a lot of money left for large amounts of insurance or savings. Mom knew she needed to go back to work. However, she had to care for me, a 5-year-old. There was also this: Mom's father died when she was not quite 4. Back then, if you were a single mother who had no one to care for your children, they went to an orphanage. Mom and her two brothers spent a few weeks there until my grandmother could arrange for her sister to care for Mom and her brothers during the day. Even though she was only in the orphanage a brief time, it left a strong memory. Mom wanted to be certain that I was not raised as a "latchkey" kid (even though that was not a term then). She took a job in a school cafeteria so she would have the same schedule and holidays that I did. It was strenuous work. She scrubbed floors and scoured pots, and I remember many evenings her being extremely tired. Even so, she found the energy to teach me what she knew about things like yardwork and home repair. She found the energy to go on all my Boy Scout outings, swim team events, and band trips. She taught me to work hard, not just in your job but in anything that you set out to do. Nothing worthwhile comes easy or fast. This was the example being set by the 55-year-old woman who would go on a 10-mile Boy Scout hike because not enough of the 40-year-old dads were available.

FAMILY IS IMPORTANT. Mom always had time when I was young for a board game or to play cards. She taught me how to play marbles and jacks. (I was the only kid my age who knew how to play these!) When I got older, she would sit in the same room with me when I played video games or did my homework, and encouraged me to watch TV with her and my grandmother. I did not understand at the time that just being together was important. Now, that is very clear. My grandmother suffered from Alzheimer's, and my mom was her primary caregiver. She lived with us for several years until she could no longer feed herself. It devastated Mom to place her in a nursing home, but she visited every day to ensure her mother was receiving proper care. I was starting high school at this point, but Mom still made all of my activities. I'll never know how she found this strength. I asked her once later in life how she did all this. Her answer: "I didn't have a choice." Again, she is the strongest person I have ever known.

PUT YOUR FAITH IN JESUS CHRIST. It was not just about going to church and being active there. Mom believed God has a plan for us. Even if we can't see or don't understand the plan, it's still there. She lived Philippians 4:6-7: "Do not be anxious about anything, but in everything, by prayer and supplication, with thanksgiving, let your requests be made known to God. And the peace of God, which surpasses all understanding, will guard your hearts and your minds in Christ Jesus." She could have been bitter about the life she had been given, but she was a woman filled with love and laughter. Her belief carried her through and brought her comfort. Mom would talk about the four important lessons I should learn from the Bible:

1. Salvation is by faith in Christ alone. It is a gift freely given by God, and we will never earn it or be worthy of it.
2. The Bible is the final authority on faith. Don't look to anything else. When in doubt, spend more time in the Word.
3. God is the sole head of the Church.
4. Everyone has equal access to God. Just talk to Him. He will answer.

Work hard. Take care of your family. Trust God. These are the values Mom taught me, and what I wanted to pass on to my children. I never saw my parents fight, and I had this idealized idea of what their marriage was. When I got married, to a woman far better than I deserve, I had all of these plans for the perfect family life. Again, sometimes God has other ideas. Katie, my oldest daughter, was diagnosed with autism when she was 3. She has severe communication problems, difficulty learning abstract concepts, poor muscle tone, and a heightened sensitivity to certain sounds. Katie "flaps" her arms and may scream or cry out for no clear reason. However, she is smart, brave, and funny. She has taught me these additional lessons about being a parent that I would never have expected:

BE PATIENT. This seems obvious but is completely different in a special-needs situation. When someone has a learning disability, you learn that tasks are not about completion. They are about building long-term skills and deductive reasoning. If Katie and I were folding laundry, it wasn't about getting the job done, but about teaching her how a shirt folds differently than pants. It's realizing that even though a task would be faster if I did it myself, Katie needs to do it even if she continues to fail. As a parent, it is SO hard to watch your children struggle. However, doing difficult tasks for them may make them happy today, but it does not prepare them for tomorrow.

DON'T SWEAT THE SMALL STUFF. And most of it is small stuff. I see friends with neuro-typical kids getting upset that their kid didn't make the select ball team, or didn't get all A's in school. I try to be sympathetic, but I struggle to relate. Part of Katie's condition is her body does not tell her when she is full, and she would eat until she would throw up. She would wait until the last possible moment to tell us that she had to go to the bathroom, and we would often not make it in time. We have learned and adapted. We taught Katie to read portion sizes on labels. Part of her condition drives her to follow rules exactly, so serving sizes have taught her portion control. (If the label says "six chips," that's all she eats! I wish I had that kind of control!) Her condition also drives her to crave schedules, so we learned to plan meals and bathroom breaks. This has given us a coping mechanism. Katie is 25 now, and things are much better. There were times, however, when just getting out to dinner and home without an accident or a meltdown was a HUGE win. Comparatively, a lot of other concerns seemed less important to me.

TAKE JOY IN THE EVERYDAY. Every minor victory is a huge win. While these are enjoyable with Katie, I also take incredible joy in my daughter Anna. She is neuro-typical, and four years younger than Katie. I was overjoyed every time Anna would bring home an art project or show me her finished homework or get an award in school. This was not typical for our family. Anna has now grown into a young woman, and we can have conversations on topics that I will never have with Katie. Most parents will never understand the joy I experience when Anna asks me questions about world events, investing, or planning for her career after college. Every day is a blessing!

I hope I pass all these lessons on to my children. They are also reminders to myself when I feel weak or sad. Be patient. Work hard. Take care of your family. See the joy around you. Don't stress out. Above all, trust God. Simple, but hard sometimes. When in doubt, I look back to the examples Mom set, as she was the best dad I've ever seen.

John Burk | Some of the Best Dads Are Moms

John Burk was born and raised in Florissant, Mo. He attended Washington University where he has a Bachelor of Science degree in Environmental Engineering and Master's degrees in Business Administration and Information Management. He is a U.S. Army veteran, and has worked the past 27 years for a company that provides technology for sulfuric acid plants (John says this is a conversation killer at parties.) He has been married to his wife Jennifer for 27 years, and they have two children. In his spare time, he competes in IronMan triathlons and has an extensive comic book collection. He knows nothing about professional sports, but if you want to talk about Batman or Star Trek, he's your guy.

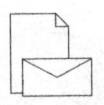

Jody Read

Being a Man In a Boy's World

Today, there are a lot of males who think they are men but really haven't built a life that represents what a true man is. Just because a guy reaches a certain age or is big and strong doesn't make him a man. A man is defined by how he thinks and acts.

I have been blessed to have the best parents, a great dad as a role model, a mom who stood by him through everything, brothers who support each other, the love of a great woman, and to be the father of three great boys and three great girls. That doesn't mean I'm perfect or raised perfect kids. I've failed them, and they've failed themselves, but it's not about winning. It's about what you do when you fail. Building your life around Godly principles and showing others that you stand for something is what matters.

Raising a family in my dad's era was easier because the social concept promoted family and community. They had their own struggles, but they had role models they could turn to for direction. People came together as families and communities to build a better world, and we held each other accountable. Unfortunately, that has largely changed. Now, it seems to be more about self-promotion and self-gratification — getting the most for yourself and building your happiness about yourself is the norm.

The secret to happiness eludes many guys out there. Yes, they can get short-term gratification through relationships, hookups, sports, acquiring possessions, and fame, but those are fleeting. These worldly things can easily be taken away through no fault of our own. No one who is dying ever says they wished they had more things; they wish for more time to fill themselves, to make a difference, and to let others around them know how they really feel about them.

Being a man is about giving all of yourself to God, to your significant other or spouse, your family, friends, and everyone around you. Fortunately, I believe my boys have learned how to be men through my example and the example of the dads in our family. They have learned it's OK to struggle, to be beaten down, to hurt but never give up, to keep improving, and never lose sight of what God placed you here to do. My grandfather used to say to me, "Can't, never could!" He learned that from his father, who grew up during the Depression as a poor farmer trying to make a living the best he knew how. I heard stories about how he gave up his inheritance to his three brothers because he didn't want to argue with them. He believed God and family were the only important things. At his funeral, the preacher told the story that, of the four brothers, only my great-grandfather had descendants. He now has more than 100 descendants. The pastor asked those attending, "Who got the real inheritance?"

My daughters are facing a world full of boys, but are looking for real men. My oldest daughter found a wonderful guy in high school who came from a great family raised on Christian values. His father exudes ethics and has taught his family well. I couldn't ask for a better son-in-law; he's a strong, patient, and caring person raising great kids. My other daughters have struggled to find the right guy because I believe society has changed, and many boys today seem to be more self-absorbed and not quite ready to be men who can lead their families and better their communities.

It's Now a Boy's World

Many boys in society today were raised by caring and devoted parents who wanted the best for them but, in a lot of cases, never let them struggle to get what they wanted. Parents giving their kids the latest of everything and doting on them for all their needs and desires has created boys who have no concept of earning money outside of their parents and don't care about the cost of getting what they want. I was raised to believe that if I wanted something, I had to earn it. I had all my needs taken care of, but if I wanted something else, I had to work for it. There were needs, and there were wants. I picked up bottles and returned them to the store so I could buy models and toys. I shined shoes, mowed grass, and picked peanuts, watermelons, peaches, and tobacco to earn money before I was old enough to drive. I wasn't given a car; I earned money for a down payment, and my dad cosigned a loan at the bank for my used pickup truck. I dated my wife in that truck, and I was proud of it, and it showed how I took care of it. Other kids in my class were given cars and trucks that they never took care of.

Today's kids often have instant access to what they want, and that's why many young adults are heavily in debt. Today, we have a TV in every room, and everyone has a cell phone. My first job out of college was working for a major worldwide electronics company, and we were some of the first field personnel to get mobile devices for our cars. We were the coolest guys around, and, yes, I actually carried the five-pound cell phone called "the brick." It cost similar to what they cost today, but unlike today's smartphones, it only made phone calls. Now, we have access to instant data at our fingertips and can get anything delivered from anywhere in the world in a matter of days. My parents saved their entire lives for a trip to Hawaii, and I did it in my 20s. Many never understand the struggle people had to go through to provide them with the life they live today.

Each generation builds upon the last generation, and life has become easier with the passing of time, but that comes with a cost. My dad was the first in our family to own a car. He then gave it to his dad when he went off to the army. My mom and dad honeymooned at my uncle's house because they couldn't afford a trip. With no college degree, my dad became the president of several banks and obtained his real estate, insurance, and appraiser licenses. I never remember going without, but I had to earn the extra. Nothing gained in this world without pain and struggle lasts or is truly a treasure. Jesus talked about what a man's heart desires, there is his treasure.

Men are to be tough but also gentle and caring, just as in the image of Jesus and God. God has shown He could be strong and stern when dealing with sin but also forgiving. Men were created to be strong and protect the ones they love from any adversity. Our society teaches that bad guys abuse people, and heroes stand up for the oppressed. Oppressors are seen as the strong getting what they want from the weak, taking advantage of others to get ahead, no matter who it hurts.

Society often promotes the outward appearance of boys' bodies and looks to say they are men. Having six-pack abs or being huge with muscles doesn't make you a man. It's what's inside that counts. When you look at elite fighting forces, it's not the tall, muscle-bound guys who make up the proficient fighting forces. It's the guys built for stamina over the long hikes in and out of hostile terrain that make the cut. Guys willing to lay down their lives for their friends and family at any moment are considered to be the elite.

Our current culture is also so fixated on "bad boys." We're taught that only guys willing to break laws, hurt people, show no remorse, and live only for today are to be looked up to. These guys are the real losers and won't be remembered. People only remember the guys who made a positive difference, even if they weren't perfect. History remembers the guys that were truly there for others. A great example is Keanu Revees, the actor in the "John Wick" and "Matrix" action films and so many others. Even though he's a great actor and makes a lot of money, he is extremely humble and goes out of his way to talk to strangers and the homeless. He's given a lot of his money to charities or to people behind the scenes in the making of movies so that they are appreciated. He doesn't do this to get publicity but to be a better person.

So, What Is a Real Man?

A real man is someone who puts others before himself. Soldiers fighting for our freedom, police officers, and firefighters who risk their own lives to keep us safe. Dads who put in long hours to provide for their families. Selfless dads who sacrifice to spend time with their kids, teaching them sports or crafts and supporting them when they fail. These are real men!

Real men are not the guys who play with people's emotions, bully others, or hold things over people. Real men know they are loved by their families and friends for what they stand for and their actions. Real men own up for their mistakes and learn how to be better. Real men ask themselves, "What can I do to improve my station in life? How can I be a better person, better father, better husband, better leader?" In life, if you're not moving positively forward, you're going backward. Your spouse and your family need to see you moving forward so they feel safe and secure knowing you'll be a better person. Life can beat you down, and the evil one is always waiting to see you stumble so he can keep you down. Keep looking up to Jesus, who is always there to be an inspiration during tough times.

Jody Read | Being a Man In a Boy's World

Jody Read is married to his high school sweetheart, Edith, who is the love of his life. Jody is the father to three girls and three boys, with seven grandchildren. Family is the most important thing in his life besides God and Edith. He is also the CEO of Sapphire Disinfection Products, located in Lake Butler, Fla. He worked for several Fortune 50 companies before starting his own company in 1998, and it grew to 365 employees. Jody sold it in 2017 and then started Sapphire to help prevent infections from viruses and bacteria. He coached his boys in baseball at Lake St. Louis, Mo. and is a St. Louis Cardinals fan. He continues to coach his grandkids in Florida with tee-ball. He and Edith are active in their community through the Rotary Club, county and city government, and church volunteering. Jody has a passion for service and enjoys helping others achieve their goals.

Mike Baue

I Love You a Thousand Times

"Have I ever told you I love you?"

"Yeah, Dad. Duh ... Only a thousand times."

"OK, good. And don't forget, I love you!"

"DAD!"

I don't remember my dad telling me that. He showed me along the way, and there are special memories, but dads back then didn't seem to say it much. The memories will stick, so will the letdowns, and that's why I'm writing you this note. My childhood was filled with many of the same things yours is, and it seemed to last forever—baseball, track, Scouts, motorcycles, camping, all the things. A million memories are packed in this balding head, and I promise it's not just a hat rack. When you grow up, God willing, you won't lose your memories. They shape your foundation of belief, success, failure, opportunity, connection, love, and faith. It seems like a lot and may be intimidating, but people tend to go further than they think they can if they decide to. They learn more. Once you begin filling up your life, you realize each experience leads to another. And that leads me to the most important thing you should write down. Here goes ...

Write a Vision for your life.

Yeah, even as a kid, write down what you'd like your life to be. If you love playing baseball, write it down. If you love hiking, write it down. Write down all the things that light you up! All the things that get you excited. Write them down. Trust me on this ...

Writing them down does something magical in your mind and heart. It's more than just thinking or saying them. It makes your mind more efficient and helps you focus on the important stuff. There's an old saying, "What you think about you do. What you do, you become." So, write down the stuff that lights you up, and it will help you develop a life that lights you up and even others around you!

Having a Vision puts power behind your goals. Now, don't overthink what I'm telling you, kiddo. You don't have to have it all figured out. Let's say right now you LOVE playing baseball. Good. Write it down, and every day, you can go out and play. Give it your all and play to win! But one day, you might decide that baseball isn't your thing anymore. Sure, that sounds crazy because it's ... BASEBALL!!! But it's true that people change. And when that happens, all you have to do is update your Vision. Grab an eraser and change it. And that leads me to the most important thing you should write down:

It's OK to change plans!

That's the thing so many kids get hung up on, thinking the whole thing has to be planned out in advance. It's just not true. At least it doesn't have to be true for you. When my dad was young, the idea was to graduate high school, get the best job you could, meet a girl, raise a family, and try your best to make the best of it. There's nothing inherently wrong or right about any of that, and that's an interesting point. The idea is different now, and in many ways equally encouraging and discouraging as any other time in history. And that leads me to the most important thing you should write down.

You get to build your life the way you want it.

Here's where I tell you my favorite part of this journey. It started when I was nine years old. My best buddy in third grade invited me to his church group event. It was a ton of fun, and I kept going. I'll tell you more about the whole story another time, but suffice it to say, the church was cool. The leaders kept it fun, and the old ladies thought I was cute. Over the next three years, the stuff we learned started making sense, as much as it could to my 12-year-old self.

Anyway, I remember one Sunday morning, I felt these crazy emotions bubbling up in my gut, and I started to sweat. It was crazy! What was this silliness happening to me? Was I sick? Nope. Then, what in the world?

And as soon as it came, it went away. Back to normal. No crazy emotions, no sweat, nothing. Alrighty, then.

A few weeks later, it happened again! Crazy feelings, sweat, all the things. BUT this time there was a little tear burbling up in my left eye. Why the left eye, no clue. But that's what it was. It just didn't make sense. And it went away again.

You need to know this, though, that I had been going to church on Sundays and Wednesday nights for a few years by then, and that's a lot of study, prayer, and hope setting in! My family didn't go to church, but I did. The youth leader came to get me and dropped me off all the time. It was really cool.

So, here's a quick little side lesson, kiddo. The more you are exposed to something, the more you tend to absorb it. So be careful what you put in your mind and heart. Be cautious of what you see. You can't unsee it!

So, a few weeks later it happened again. Feeling, sweat, tears. Yes ... MORE TEARS. I had NO idea why. But there was one thing different. I didn't see this coming. If you gave me a bajillion dollars, I would never have guessed what happened next!

My feet started wiggling. Toes tapping. The preacher invited anyone who wants to accept Christ as their personal savior to come forward and accept Him. It was like magic, or something … Like I was watching from outside my body. My body began moving. I was WALKING FORWARD. WHAT!!!! HOW!!!! WAIT!!!

I walked forward, bawling like a baby. For real. It was an ugly snot cry. You should've seen it. I'm sobbing, who knows why, men and women are praying, the congregation is singing and clapping, and, man, I let it out. I cried, cried, and cried. After what seemed like 50 years (probably five or six minutes), my breathing started to calm. The tears began to dry. My body was spent, and I was confused. I accepted Christ as my savior!!! No one ever told me exactly what it was going to feel like. But that's probably best. I wouldn't have believed them. There I was, standing in front of the whole church as a new Christian!

Here I am all these years later, and I can assure you it hasn't been easy. Life can be hard. But having Jesus as my savior, healer, guide, companion, and friend has been the, well, let me say it like this... my greater desire for your life is to draw near to Jesus. That leads me to the most important thing you should write down:

As your relationship with Jesus grows, you begin to love with what He loves, and to do what He desires of you.

That's called sanctification. Drawing nearer to Christ, and further from sin. You start loving what He loves, and the stuff He doesn't becomes less appealing. The things that light you up are more in alignment with His will for your life. It can be confusing, and it was for me at 12 years old. But what happened was real, it was exciting, and it stuck with me. It will with you, too.

As you write your Vision for your life, you'll start seeing things in a new way. New opportunities arise from out of nowhere. They start with a foundation of love, joy, peace, patience, kindness, goodness, faithfulness, gentleness, and self-control. Sounds like a lot of adult stuff, I know. But it's not just for grownups. I mean, look at us. Do you have any questions about all this?

Nope!

I have one for you ...

"Have I ever told you I love you?"

"DAD!"

Mike Baue is a husband, father, pastor, entrepreneur, musician, and pilot. Growing up in a farming community helped instill a strong system of values. After a decade of playing music professionally, he decided to shift into business, and now owns OsteoStrong Franchises and a real-estate holding company.

In his early 40s, Mike felt a calling to ministry, which was a defining factor in everything to come. His desire is to glorify God and to share the love of Christ.

Within his professional and spiritual pursuits, Mike finds joy in flying, riding motorcycles, teaching, coaching, and nurturing business growth. Together with his wife, Christine, Mike cherishes the adventures of parenthood, raising four children who share their passion for music, travel, family gatherings, and the charming chaos of raising chickens.

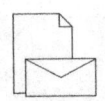

Bobby Christopher

A Beaming Girl-Dad

I have been given numerous blessings in my 42 years, but none more rewarding than being a father to my three beautiful daughters. I never envisioned a future with daughters. I always pictured my future with a beautiful wife and twin linebacker boys named Blaine and Cage. Fortunately, I did end up with my beautiful wife. The Lord blessed my wife and me with girls in lieu of twin boys. I could not imagine my life any other way.

Twenty years ago, it was hard even to imagine having a future at all. I was an "invincible" man serving in the United States Marine Corps as a gunner/machine gunner preparing for deployment to Fallujah, Iraq. It was ingrained in every Marine that the mission is first and Marines are expendable. There is not a Marine whom I deployed with that would not have laid his life down for mine or an innocent civilian. We were all prepared to die.

My life was forever changed by our deployment to Fallujah in 2005. A wise platoon sergeant told me, "Be careful what you wish for because a war will change a man." That was his response as I complained about our unit not being called up for deployment about a year before receiving orders for Fallujah.

The deployment taught me valuable life lessons: Be thankful for what we have and don't take things for granted. There are vivid memories that will be with me forever, and as a result, my loved ones are closest to me. They are left dealing with the remnants in the form of anger or depression at times.

I decided to write this testimony for my daughters, who know I served in the Marine Corps and that I was met with close calls in Iraq. They, however, don't know how much it affects my ability to effectively communicate with them, nor have they ever heard in great detail the sequence of events that I still refuse to allow to define me as a father.

On July 19 and September 19, 2005, I was hit with "improvised explosive devices (IED)" near Fallujah. I am convinced divine intervention occurred on that September day as the blast from the enemies' 155mm tank round was detonated, which is why I am still alive today.

That September morning had a different feel to it, as that day marked the last day of our last mission of that deployment. We had spent the previous nine months embracing the suck. We knew we would begin decompressing on base, and once we handed off our gear to the unit ripping through with us, we would be done and flying back to the States in the coming weeks.

My platoon was tasked with escorting fuel trucks and tanks down a stretch of road we had traveled numerous times before. As we began to get closer to a known hotbed area, that same platoon sergeant came over the radio and said, "Gunners, maintain a low profile with your heads on a swivel. Don't get complacent." It was just seconds later that the IED was detonated.

As the heavy blast ripped through, chaos ensued. My driver went by "ABM" (Angry Black Man — Martin McClung). For 95 percent of our deployment, he sat to the right of me in the rear passenger seat behind the vehicle commander as one of our "dismount Marines." For this mission, and this mission only, we had only four people in our Humvee, which included our interpreter Muhammed. He had been sitting where ABM usually would have.

As the hot metal ripped through the right side of the vehicle, Muhammed was in the most direct line of fire. ABM was hit with shrapnel in the hand and my vehicle commander, Dallas, in much of his upper body. Muhammed suffered the brunt of the blast. He lost a leg and an arm but ultimately survived with the help of a timely medivac.

As for me, there is absolutely no reason I should be writing this today. It is nearly impossible to put this into words and provide an accurate description of why I say this was "divine intervention," but here goes.

I was a TOW Gunner, which stands for Tube Launched Optically Tracked Wire Guided Missile System. Due to the size and length of the missile system, gunners who shoot TOW missiles do not have any protection above the Humvee. My setup consisted of a TOW system facing to the rear of my Humvee as my primary weapon, which was a 240 Gulf, and faced to about 11 o'clock as we staggered our weapons to flank the left and the right of the convoy as we moved.

A bomb with the power of a 155mm tank round was detonated less than 8 feet from my vehicle with a perfectly timed strike. This blast was large enough to completely blow off my welded gun mount on the front of my Humvee. Shrapnel flew through our doors and was embedded in the right side of our Coleman ice chest. This shrapnel, being just an inch or two away from hitting my leg, likely would have been fatal for me.

If someone had been there to take a photo, it would have captured an angel shielding me. I have thought of a prayer as we were being medically transferred to Fallujah. This prayer consisted of many thanks being given to Jesus along with many promises I had made in that prayer.

I have always had the question of, "Why me?" Why did God spare me? Why did I walk away alive and with relatively minor issues compared to Muhammed? I believe I was given another chance at life so I would have the opportunity to help raise my three girls, who are destined to do great things.

I only include my background because it does affect me more than I ever thought. It affects me more than it did 19 years ago. All of this has complicated how I communicate with my girls. This is not a pity party, nor is it a call for help. It is just my attempt for my girls to hear fatherly advice from someone who does not express good advice nearly enough.

To my first-born Olivia, who will turn 16 this year:
In 2008, you made me the proudest father. When you were born, I could not wait to show you off to your grandparents. I brought you out to my dad with tears in my eyes, saying that Kristen just gave birth to the most beautiful girl ever.

I knew you were going to be special. Little did I know that you would continue to impress me even more as time went by. You are an incredible athlete. I am not a, "My kid is getting a scholarship" parent, but I also know with your work ethic and drive that you can most definitely play college ball.

What impresses me most is your ability to shine after you face adversity. You tore an ACL at 12 and the other ACL at 14. Most kids would have given up or taken a break, but you continued to juggle soccer balls, shoot baskets, run, lift, and continued to show up to practices and games you couldn't play to support your teams. You are a competitor, and you refuse to give anything less than your all. I enjoy watching you do what you love to do because it makes you happy and because it gives me a glimpse of the greatness you will offer the world as you become an adult.

Academically, you have been a straight-A student. I don't understand how you can play sports at the level you do and still find time to study and maintain a 4.1 GPA.

Whatever you do in life, you don't need to be perfect. Keep being you and doing your best, but don't put too much pressure on yourself. Just be the best YOU you can be.

To Sloane, my middle child who will turn 12 this year:

From the day you were born, we knew you would be one of a kind. You have such a fiery personality and a kind heart. Much like your older sister, you are athletic, and you play your sports with passion and aggrensity (aggressive-intensity). I enjoy watching you play and sprinting to every ball, and your confidence to take every open shot available.

You have impressed me by just being you. You have your own swag and style that matches your personality. Don't compare yourself to others or get pulled into peer pressure. You are my strong-willed, fun-loving 12-year-old. I have told my friends and coworkers that you will be the President of the United States one day. Continue to do the right things, make good decisions, and go after your goals!

To Blake, my youngest daughter, who will turn eight this year:

You are our miracle child. You were given to us after we thought we could not have any more kids, and we could not be more blessed to have you in our family. I have watched you in all aspects of life, and you continue to be the most caring, fun-loving, compassionate 7-year-old I have ever met.

I cannot wait to see what God has planned for your life. You spread joy to everyone around you. Whether you continue further in gymnastics, basketball, or school clubs, I cannot wait to watch every moment of it. I hope it is basketball you choose because there is nothing better than watching you run baseline to baseline while smiling from ear to ear!

To all my girls, I leave this:
- Re-establish our priorities and live life for Jesus.
- Love more and fight less.
- Do the right thing even when everyone else is doing wrong.
- Work less and spend more time with our family and friends.
- Be a better version of yourself tomorrow than you are today.

Bobby Christopher | A Beaming Girl-Dad

Bobby Christopher is a construction professional in the St. Louis market and currently serves as the operations director for Wright Construction Services. He is a Purple Heart Combat Veteran who served in Operation Iraqi Freedom while serving in the United States Marine Corps and currently serves as board president for the Mid-American Veterans Museum, where he is passionate about improving the lives of local veterans and their families and ensuring that their stories and legacies live on.

Bobby is the husband of Kristen and is the proud father of his three daughters: Olivia, Sloane, and Blake. He enjoys his role in raising his daughters and shares in their passion for sports, traveling, and living life to the fullest.

Steve Koskela

A Busy Dad's Perspective

I often wonder, "Where has the time gone?" How was that already two years ago, five years ago, 20 years ago? The days seem to race by. Minutes become hours, hours become days, days become weeks, and before you know it, your oldest daughter is 15, and you are looking for her first car. I often struggle with time management, committing time to the most important things in this short life. I would ultimately waste our precious, finite time with our family and friends on the unimportant. I have compiled my thoughts as a busy father of three daughters, a husband, a leader in the workplace and community, and a man learning to be better every day.

Often, I find myself trying to make time for my wife or making time for my kids. I try to "fit" them into MY schedule between the tasks I have for work for MY commitments to the community or things I thought I wanted to do. My priorities were so far out of whack that I was squeezing in tiny moments in MY busy schedule for what was most important. I needed to ground myself and realign what was most important to me. I had to really assess the opportunities presented to me, especially those that would be a considerable time commitment. I take on too much, try to do too many things, and rob my family and myself of quality time together. I had to learn the power of saying, "No, thank you." I've decided to start making time for everything else. Prioritizing family has been paramount in my life for a multitude of reasons. My family is my cornerstone of support, love, joy, stability, and emotional security. Amidst all of life's challenges and uncertainties, family remains my constant source of comfort and guidance. Family is where I find my irreplaceable significance, important to all men. We have a desire for significance; we long to be needed. There is no one who needs you more than your family. I promise you: Work will write your help-wanted ad before your obituary is published. Would your family move on so quickly?

I try to focus on not wasting time. We don't have enough of it, and don't get to ask for more when it is our time to meet our maker. Time has a way of escaping us with the distractions present today. In an era dominated by technology and access to immediate information, it is easy to squander hours in a week, even in a day, on the phone, tablet, or in front of the TV. Despite my best intentions, the constant pings of notifications and the temptation to check emails, social media feeds, or binge-watch shows encroaches upon valuable time that I should be devoting to meaningful interactions with my loved ones or time I could be focusing on self-improvement.

I often find myself disconnected from the present moment and killing the quality of my time with my family. Being present with the family is one of my focused goals. I want to be in the moment with them, rather than reading about someone else's sandwich that they had at a new café four hours from me, presenting zero real significance to my life. Just because I am physically spending time with my family, I constantly remind myself to be present for them mentally and emotionally. A great friend of mine always uses the phrase, "Be where your feet are." It seems easy in theory, right? Of course, I am where my feet are. Yet, I consistently find my mind in a different place — usually still at work or thinking about what I "should" be doing and not focusing on the smiles, tears, or needs of my wife and daughters and scrolling a social media platform instead of intently watching their sporting events and reading emails instead of talking to my wife. The list goes on.

All these distractions rob me of true joy, but more importantly, rob my family of the joy the moment could have presented them. It dawned on me when I missed an amazing play that my daughter made in one of her soccer games. She immediately looked over to the sideline for praise and support to find me looking down at my phone, not present for her in that moment. The smile and happiness immediately left her face as if it were almost better if I hadn't been there. At least there wouldn't have been the disappointment or that feeling of insignificance that she had to feel at that moment. I spent the entire day apologizing to her for missing it and trying to make it up to her, and she graciously forgave me as our kids always do ... But I couldn't forgive myself. It still hurts, and I had to learn from it. That emotion I felt for disappointing my kids was far worse than the "I'm not mad, I'm just disappointed" speeches I would get from my dad when I was a boy.

I have embraced the "be where your feet are" mindset in all my daily activities, including work. I have found tremendous success and have been able to save some of that precious time in my work life, as well. Being present at the moment has increased my awareness of my team's needs and gratitude for what they do from being able to witness and be fully a part of it. My connections with them have strengthened. Having a leader who is always preoccupied with something outside the organization is like having no leader. I am now able to approach challenges with clarity and intentionality. I no longer have to worry or stress about challenges that I know nothing about but have been presenting themselves for a significant amount of time. In practicing the principle of being where our feet are, we free ourselves from the burden of unnecessary stress and anxiety, allowing us to approach those challenges with resilience and perspective since we are truly present.

Worry and anxiety have always taken a considerable amount of my time. Worry is present in all of us. While a certain level of concern can be natural and even beneficial, allowing worry to consume us leads to a cycle of unproductive, wasted time. Excessive worry squanders precious moments on scenarios that may never come to pass or over which we have little control. Engaging in worry not only drains our mental and emotional energy but also detracts from our ability to focus on productive pursuits. I think it is like spinning one's wheels in the mud, expending effort without making any progress. Time spent worrying is time lost to enjoying the present moment, pursuing meaningful goals, and fostering personal growth. Usually, on something we have no control over! That's what we naturally do as dads... We worry! I urge you to focus on the things you can control. Tackle those challenges. If the concerns are outside of the circle of your control, time spent dwelling or worrying about those "things" is time wasted. How we cope with worry and anxiety is something we all work on or handle in different ways.

My escape from worry and anxiety, apart from prayer, is physical activity. Physical activity is a natural remedy for stress. "How do I make time for that?" Glad you asked … Do it early! Trust me, you will be in such a better mood throughout the day. A few years ago, I joined a group of men, just as busy as me, going through the same challenges of life, for a men's workout called F3 — fitness, fellowship, faith. We get up at 5:00 a.m. before the day has begun and get the physically hard part out of the way together. Early morning workouts have many health benefits for me, including better sleep at night and less stress throughout the day from the "feel good" neurotransmitter release of endorphins. Still, also physical activity doubles as a distraction from anxious thoughts. I can't dwell on the things stressing me out if I am focused on catching my breath and lifting heavy things. It aligns my mind for the day. If I can get up early and complete that hard physical workout, I can take on anything! The other obvious benefit of getting up early and doing the activity is that I am not removing quality time from my wife and kids. Afternoons and evenings are for them. Not only do I get it done while they are still asleep, but I also set an example of fitness and self-improvement and make myself the best version of myself.

Time is so precious. Spend the majority of your time on the ones you love. Make them your priority. Build your relationships with your family with honest and purposeful conversations, undistracted. Build them with love and quality time. Why waste time on worry? Why take on more if it takes away from your limited time with them? We don't know how much of it we have and don't get to ask for more.

Steve Koskela | A Busy Dad's Perspective

Steve Koskela was born and raised until his early teen years in Florissant, Mo., to Steve and Shannon Koskela. Steve and his brother, Matt, had a modest childhood in a neighborhood filled with children their age who they could play with outside until their mom yelled for them to get home.

In 1999, Steve's family moved to the City of O'Fallon. A 2002 graduate of Fort Zumwalt West High School, Steve found his love for construction and management practices in multiple afterschool activities. After attending Lindenwood University and Ranken Technical College, Steve met his wife of 15 years, Jenni. They have been blessed with three incredible daughters.

Steve is the vice president of operations for a large installation distributor of building products and a current City Councilman for O'Fallon. He enjoys being in the great outdoors with his family, helping coach his daughters in their numerous sports, playing softball, drinking bourbon, and following Formula 1 racing.

Steve discovered his faith in late 2022. Praising the Lord for the blessings received and salvation through His grace is at the heart of his daily activities.

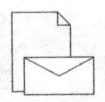

Jerry Krnotch

A Dad's Promise

Hey boy, I know it's been a while since we've spoken. I hope this note finds you well.

I know our last time together didn't end pleasantly. It seems we both had some sore feelings we'd been allowing to fester, and they all finally became exposed. It worries your mother and me when we don't hear from you. We both know you need to find your own way in this life, but this doesn't ease our concern for your well-being at all. Not communicating with us makes it even more concerning; it allows me to understand a bit how my own father must have felt when I did the same thing back when I was your age.

You see, your mother and I have known each other since we were in kindergarten. She was my best friend and we both lived in the same small town, on the same country road, and went to the same school and took the same school bus. As we grew, we also grew fonder of one another and found ourselves going from grade school playmates to high school sweethearts. Some of the best memories of my entire life are those made with your momma by my side.

I loved her from the day we met. I had secretly planned our future together in my daydreams. She, too, would fantasize with me about us one day living together in a castle, or on a farm, or moving to some far-off exotic place that most others from our little backwoods town couldn't dream of. That was and still is much of why I loved her so, because she was able to see so much possibility in life when everyone else seemed to think things were simply meant to stay the same.

Summer after summer, we ran through those hills and valleys without serious care in the world, getting home in time for supper and being sure her pony at home was taken care of. That's all we worried about. We tried our best to be good Christian kids as our parents commanded, though from time to time, our teenage angst got the better of us. We were happy, and life was simple and relatively easy in those days now that I look back upon it.

Many years of childhood, however, gave way to our senior year of high school and the prospect of new beginnings in our adult lives. Not many in our area could hope for college or moving away to something bigger. Still, your momma's parents did their best to ensure she had some way to escape a life of relative poverty and an opportunity for a better life. Being from a place where not much ever changed and having an adventurous heart, she was very excited to venture out on her own and attend university. Funding was nowhere to be found for me, however, so this meant she would be traveling several hours away for school while I was staying near home. This was a painful time for both of us, and we both agreed, after trying for several months, that a long-distance relationship was not easy and wasn't working out. I tried to convince her to marry me and promised we would figure things out, but we ultimately agreed in the end that we should break up and find our separate ways. Neither of us dealt with this separation well; we wouldn't come to realize this until sometime later.

I often thought of your mother. Getting to know any other girl was difficult. None of them were her, and therefore, they were not right for me.

I hadn't heard anything from her since we split up for college and heard she became engaged to another guy. I started to let go. I was becoming comfortable with my bachelor life and decided if she was no longer to be mine, then at least she was going to be happy, so I would be relatively happy, too.

One evening, though, I was surprised when my phone rang, and I heard a very familiar voice at the other end — one that sent every emotion I knew how to feel rushing through me. It was your mother. She had gotten my number from a mutual friend of ours who ran an auto parts store that I visited a lot. I didn't know what to say. I think I even sat there for a minute before replying to her. She had been in town for a few weeks and wanted to know if she could come visit me. Before I could come up with a reason why she couldn't, I heard myself saying *yes* and giving her my address. She was on her way.

Part of me thought she was coming back to break my heart again and that I should just send her away. Another part hoped she was coming to ask me to take her back and that everything would be as happy as it was before she left once more. I knew, however, to just keep it cool and treat this like a friendly visit; no need to get emotional after all. I have learned to manage that over the past two years.

She arrived, and we started with small talk, of course. I offered her a beer, and she said *no*. Neither one of us was even old enough to drink, but beer was all I had in the fridge (that and some ketchup).

After about an hour of small talk, she told me the guy she was engaged with had left her for another girl. She had been split up with him for about four months and had come to grips with the fact that she was not truly happy with him to begin with. She was living a life that was fake and not who she truly wanted to be. But then she told me the real news: She was pregnant, about four months along. And the father of the child wanted nothing to do with her or the baby.

I was in complete shock, every fiber of my being wanted to run away from that situation, but at the same time, I was still so in love with her that I could not dream of saying anything angrily to her or turning her away. She wasn't there to ask me to step in; she was there to apologize for breaking my heart after realizing later that what we had was something few people ever get a chance to experience. And like a cheesy romance movie, I told her that if she wanted, I would take care of her and stand beside her every step of the way. She was still my love and my childhood best friend.

When you were born, I was by her side every step of the way. We brought you home, and I made a promise to be your daddy, no matter what that took. Shortly after you arrived, your mother asked me to marry her. It was not common in our day for the woman to ask the man, but I, of course, said *yes* without hesitation.

We were married a couple of months later in a small ceremony at a VFW hall, and all our family and friends came with food to share. We had no honeymoon. It was straight back to work for me the next day; I now had a family to support. I made a promise to both her and you to be the best husband and father I could, and to provide all the opportunities for you that I was never afforded because we could never afford it.

A few years later, your sister arrived. You were a bit jealous at first, but she followed you like a puppy dog as soon as she could crawl, and the two of you became best buddies. We were two young parents with a boy and a girl at church every Sunday, doing the best we could to teach you both right from wrong and instilling the best moral compass we knew.

It was when you had reached the age of 12 that we decided we should tell you about your biological father. This conversation was private, just you, me, and your mother. You were very confused but ended the conversation by hugging me as hard as you could. You held on for several minutes, which made me feel like you truly understood that I was your daddy because I chose to be and that this would never change. It was a good feeling that day. You never asked anything more about your biological father, to my relief and concern.

Now you've grown, reminding me much of the young man I was at your age, hell-bent on making your own way without help or advice from anyone. I would tell you I know exactly what you're dealing with yet, but this is still your journey, not mine. You and I started on different trails. I hope someday you can see that every choice I made was because I wanted to provide you with the best opportunities I could, opportunities I did not have available to me at your age. I made a promise to you and your mom to be your daddy, and that I am; this will never change. Please remember this.

I love you, son, and I hope you are safe. I will be your Dad always, I promise.

Dad

Jerry Krnotch | A Dad's Promise

Raised in the northern most part of Appalachia, the Southern tier of Upstate NY, Jerry Lee was part of the working class as a young boy, working every hour he wasn't at school or spending time with his childhood sweetheart. The outdoors and blue-collar lifestyle defined who he was as a kid, trying so hard to be a man.

Dreaming of a higher quality of life, yet finding few opportunities for a brighter future, hard work seemed the only path forward. A young man already grown beyond his years, Jerry Lee would now find himself faced with a much larger job, one that would push him even further into adulthood and, test his character as a man and deepen his commitment to love. He would make a promise that would change the course of his life and change the direction of his family tree toward a better future.

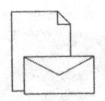

Dr. Jim Ottomeyer

Confessions of a Bad Dad

My life includes a few regrets, many overwhelming joys, and way too many close calls. Life has never been boring, and it has been incredibly enhanced by my four children. But the journey has not always been easy.

I wanted to be the best dad in the world, tend to their every bruise, cheer on their triumphs, lend a shoulder when their hearts ached. I failed. I failed big time. I let so many little distractions pull me away from so many of these moments. The grass, computer games, business, friends, community involvement … you can fill in the blanks. My life seemed so together from the outside, but inside "My World," balance was that elusive lightning bug that would flash just beyond reach. I would catch a glimpse of it and reach for it with all my speed, cunning, and might. One microsecond later, it would flicker yellow and — wait! — then another one would light up, and I would think I could catch that one. All the while, the original bug I was trying to capture would drift farther and farther away.

Balance is the hardest thing for a dad to achieve. Once you become a dad, you can no longer return to that simple existence of simply being a man. You have given that up. YOU ARE DAD! Balance is that dirty little secret we keep quiet about as dads.

My next statement is the most painful, and the most liberating, truth I have learned in my 27 years of fatherhood: I will never achieve balance.

Fortunately, I decided to ignore the pain of that truth and go on. I was not going to give up on the quest for balance. On the contrary! The battle and the journey of trying to achieve balance is what made me a better dad.

As Dad, we could easily take the well-traveled road of letting TV, sports, school, and video games play most of our roles. It's much easier to give in to those distractions than to really parent. Give in? I did. I would be lying if I said I had not fallen into those pitfalls many times. It was much easier to let others "dad" my kids instead of taking time from my video games, tee-times, nights out with the boys, and all those other lightening bugs that distracted me.

So, how do we go on when we know we have and will continue to fail? How do we win enough of the battles to make a difference in our children's lives? Looking back, I failed so many times. I can honestly say I was a "bad dad." There were so many failures I could have avoided if I had only realized that most of my personal wants were nonproductive distractions. Those wants had nothing to do with being a good dad!

In my early dad days, I frequently lied to myself about how my wants were really needs. I rationalized and found excuses for not being more patient, for not spending a little extra time with my children, and for not really listening to their pleas for attention. The horrible truth is I knew I was being a bad dad. It hurts deep within my soul for those opportunities I squandered.

Life gets in the way of good intentions. But they are still good intentions. The key is to take those good intentions and manifest them into good actions. We are all going to be bad dads at one time or another. We must aspire to keep our eyes on the original lightning bug and those good Dad intentions. Most of all, we have to avoid the distractions that pull us off the path.

Kids are always watching. They are training for life every moment of every day, and our actions are the tools they use to prepare them for their journey. My children saw me taking way too many shortcuts and not being the dad I should have been. Most importantly, they witness the balance, or lack of it, that we create in our family. They hurt when we fail, they celebrate when we succeed, and they learn from our example.

My biggest failures and regrets were my lack of attentiveness to their wants, concerns, and needs. It was easy to feel bothered when they came to me with something. There were so many times when I was not where my feet were when they needed me. My body was in the room, but my attention was not focused on them. I realize that now, and I probably knew that then, but it did not stop me from failing. They deserved better! Instead of reveling in their attention, I dwelled in my own wants. I stole their important daddy/kid time. It was important to them and should have been important to me. I showed them I was far from balanced. Everything was about me instead of being about us, about our relationships, about our family.

Family Lesson: A Fish Story

I loved trout fishing and desperately wanted to pass that passion on to my kids. We went often as a family. I remember one morning all of us standing along the shore at sunrise waiting for the whistle to sound. As soon as you heard it, everyone along the bank would drop their lines into the water. I can still feel my heart — with a palpable thud … thud … thud … — in my chest. Each thud would move us a second closer to casting our lines. I knew the fish frenzy was about to begin.

When you fish in a trout park, you cannot begin your fishing day until that whistle goes off. Those trout were released the night before and many have not eaten for days. They are innocent to the concept of a sharp metal object biting into their lip, and they will hit on anything that moves. This is the perfect time to get children interested in fishing. They are pretty much assured of catching fish. I will never forget the glow and widening of their eyes the first time they hooked into a trout. It is one of those proud daddy moments!

That morning, we all stood side by side with our poles cocked back. The ages of my children ranged from 3 to 9, and they stood like statues in tempered excitement. The whistle blew. In seconds, I latched a huge one: glory and pure adrenalin filled my veins.

Then, it happened—the 3-year-old hooked one, then the 5-year-old. My wife was frantically calling for my help. Then the other two children both hooked fish. I was struggling with my lunker (a big fish). The world grayed out around me. I heard nothing for what seemed an eternity, but what was more like 30 seconds. It was all about me. I remember thinking, *I got to get this one in. My wife can handle the kids. I have a lunker on the line!*

I had talked with the kids about what to do in this moment, going through every detail. But when their eyes lit up and widened ten times their normal size, the kids really did not know what to do. I thought it was so easy to fish. But as life usually works, the real thing is much different than any instruction Dad could give. They were not prepared, and Dad was failing them ... again. I was concerned about my wants, not their needs.

The 3-year-old snapped the line, and the fish got away. Tears, sobs, and utter defeat echoed on the bank. Snap! went the 5-year-old's line. More tears, more sobs. Then the worst thing that could happen—well, it happened. One of the older kids landed her fish.

In my family, competition rules over everything. The anarchy that ensued was indescribable. The oldest child had won. She was victorious, and her competitors were screaming and crying in defeat. It was all on me!!!

My wife was not happy with my selfishness; my children were screaming at each other. The gray fog of exhilaration was lifting in my heart. And, as if destined ... *Snap!* ... my lunker was gone. The morning was a wreck. All my good intentions of taking my family fishing had resulted in huge disappointment for almost everyone. The oldest held her fish high.

At that moment, the realization hit me. The morning, the trip, and life were not all about me. I had ruined that day and spoiled a potentially awesome moment in their lives. I turned their joy into chaos. I did not achieve balance for the rest of that day. It was a bad day for a bad dad. Hopefully, they have forgotten about that morning. I have not. Future mornings on the bank of the trout streams would be about them. I would help them catch fish to their delight. I could fish later.

This was an example of how I lost sight of the real lightning bug. My children needed me to be attentive and help them learn how to fish. I did not need to catch that lunker. I had caught many lunkers before and have caught many since. But I failed in that one moment. I was not thinking about balance. I was thinking about myself. I needed to clarify my wants and their needs.

Jessica, Jay, Lauren, Blake ... I wish I could say I was an awesome dad. We know the truth. My balance was off more than it was on. I have failed you in so many ways. I know I could have done better, and I wish I could have lived by the balance I so desired to gift to all of you! You guys are awesome, despite the failures of your dad. I love you more than life itself and can only hope my failures become your triumphs. Remember to chase the right light!

Dr. Jim Ottomeyer | Confessions of a Bad Dad

Dr. R. James Ottomeyer III has been practicing privately for over 20 years. He takes great pride in his devotion to God, his family, his country, his community, and of course, his patients

Dr. Jim was born in St. Louis, MO, where he lived until he was 8 years old. His family then moved to Cedar Rapids, IA, where he stayed until he graduated from The University of Iowa. After graduation, he returned to his hometown of St. Louis where he attended Logan University and earned a Doctorate of Chiropractic, B.S. in Life Sciences, as well as certifications in Sports Chiropractic and Acupuncture. He later received his second Doctorate in Naturopathic Medicine from John Thomas College. He is happily married 30 years to his incredible wife Kerrie and is blessed with four awesome children. Work hard.....Play Harder will be etched into his gravestone upon death.

Joshua Davis

Attack Life With Fastballs

When I was 5 years old, I threw a baseball for the first time. It was the most incredible experience I had ever had. At that moment, I discovered why I was born.

What were you born for? Do you know? Are you still searching?

As I write this, I am a 46-year-old, divorced father of a 16-year-old daughter and a 14-year-old son. I have had so many experiences from my life in general and from baseball in particular that will help me explain the points I will share. I like looking back on these moments because they opened my eyes and provide me with a path now for being a better father and a better person.

My mission here is to draw awareness to some of the biggest lessons I learned growing up. If you need to hear these words, I hope they help you find what you are seeking!

Baseball taught me that nothing is given and rewards must be earned. I lost a tournament championship game when I was 12. I had spent so much time honing my skills as a pitcher that I had developed a pretty good reputation in my area. I thought I was hot stuff and that another tournament championship game was going to be an easy task. Alas, we lost pretty badly. The tournament, however, was double elimination. I was so mad at myself for losing our first shot at the championship that

— bruised but not beaten — I asked my coach to let me pitch the next game, which immediately followed that first loss. He allowed it and that time we won! I cherished that championship so much because of how hard I worked for it.

Another example of baseball affecting my life was when it took me to Europe for two weeks when I was only 14! While there, I learned so much about the world of which I was unaware. Going to Belgium, Germany, and Amsterdam awakened me to different cultures and so much more. I learned, for instance, that in Belgium they like to put mayonnaise on French fries (lol). I will never forget how much fun I had and how having the courage to go outside my comfort zone taught me so much about the world — and myself.

Baseball taught me an additional life lesson when I was a freshman in high school. That was the first time I had to have a minimum grade-point average in order to try out for a baseball team. I failed to meet the requirement; I was so heartbroken. But this temporary setback forced me to focus my efforts on something I really didn't want to do in order to get to the one thing I really cared about. In life, we don't get to only do what we "want." We also have to take care of the many things we "need" to do; only then are we able to do the things we love.

Something else I learned about baseball is that it can pay you back. When I was a senior in high school, I was awarded a full scholarship to play baseball at Jefferson College in Hillsboro, Mo. I played there for two years (1995-97), and during that time, I made the National Dean's List for academics — I had come a long way from freshman year in high school — and was named to the 1996 NJCAA Region 16 All-Star Team. Those two years were paid for by the school and helped me grow so much as a person.

I learned how life works through these experiences. I could tell you what you should look for, what you need to do to be successful, or simply how to be happy. Ultimately, though, it comes down to what *you* think. Each one of us has a life to live that is separate from any other. Your experiences will be *your* story and will guide *your* life path. What experiences have you already had? What lessons have they taught you? Where will they take your life?

Baseball simply is a game of nine innings between two teams to see who will emerge the victor. But what life has taught me is that not only does each inning contain six outs, three for both teams, but nine long innings of adversity, situations, and strategies that ultimately are a puzzle piece in the grand picture of the overall game.

Life is the same. I hope this chapter accomplishes three things: helps you understand how to recognize your purpose, motivates you to dedicate yourself to it, and allows you to grasp the reason it fuels you.

*****

Throwing a baseball for the first time felt so right because it took so little effort. It was just … *natural*. Somehow, someway, the baseball came off my fingertips like a painter uses a paintbrush, or a musician plays a guitar. When the smallest thing feels so right, it leads you to the next step of difficulty. That process repeats over and over until you reach your limit or you advance to that next step.

For me, baseball was effortless because I loved it. I played as much as I could until my body could not continue. I strove to be the best because the challenges that drove me to improve made me feel better when I developed with each progressive step. I loved baseball so much that I was willing to sacrifice so many things to reach my potential.

The most important thing I ever sacrificed for my passion was time. When I could have been playing with my friends, riding my bike, or doing a million other things, I was in the field behind my house working on strategies that would help me improve as a player. I spent countless hours pretending to work through situations at various positions, so I would be prepared when it came time to stand in that moment. When you find your passion, you want to be your best, and you want to be THE best. That requires heartfelt dedication and sacrifice.

The sacrifice is a much different story. Life is going to put you in a position of being overwhelmed with so many different things that you may sometimes lose sight of your true passion. You will be bombarded with variables you didn't even know existed until they get in the way of your dreams. Sometimes, we have to work through the daily grind and put our dreams on hold. The disappointing fact for so many of us, though, is we allow our vision to get clouded by other variables that take us away from the pursuit of our dreams. Throughout my life, I have learned that when I allowed the outside variables to distract my attention, I grew further and further away from my dream of becoming a professional baseball player. Sometimes, you have to say *no* to the good so you can obtain the great!

Oddly, the biggest struggle I faced as a young athlete was success. My natural ability seemed far better than my competitors. That cultivated a false sense of security that made me feel too comfortable with my abilities. Don't let that happen to you. No matter your capabilities or how much better you may be than your peers, you have to approach every day with the same mindset that you can improve. Do not take anything for granted, and do not allow yourself to be told by the world that you are good just the way you are. Every day, you have the opportunity to be better and to show that you will not get left behind by the lack of drive to improve.

Why all the work, the struggle, the sacrifice? What is the payoff in the end? Only you know that answer and only you will understand your reasons why. For me, it was knowing that my efforts were validated through my achievements and how rewarding it was to stand above another because of my dedication. All of it was justified because I had overcome the challenges of adversity.

When I look back over my career, I see that I have been continually developing myself not only as a competitor but as a person. This ever-changing world systematically goes on day by day, week by week, month by month, and year by year, just like baseball. It takes being a part of something bigger than you as an individual as well as working and sacrificing for the purpose of seeing and realizing your capabilities. Are you aware of yours? Have you been tested enough? Are you sacrificing enough?

Life is relentless; life is not going to give up. So, find your purpose. When you do, the sacrifices will seem effortless, the challenges manageable. There will be light at the end of the tunnel, and that light will be a better you.

So many of us find ourselves complacent because it is comfortable. That feeling leads us to day-by-day struggles because our complacency acts like an anchor, holding us in place while the world grows around us and, in essence, leaves us behind. Don't get left behind! You are the only one who can make that choice, and I hope you make it. You are capable of great things.

Dig deep within yourself and find what it is that fills your heart with so much joy and passion that causes everything else to fade away. That is what will drive you to greatness and what will lead you to a life of fulfillment. Your accomplishments will feel like they were achieved with minimal effort because you so willingly gave to the cause.

And all of this is only the beginning of your capabilities. Go earn the life you want through hard work, dedication, and passion.

God bless!

Joshua Davis | Attack Life With Fastballs

Joshua Davis was born and raised in the St. Louis area by two amazing parents who taught him right from wrong, good character traits, and to lean on his heart and faith for guidance.

During his childhood, Joshua found a passion for baseball and gave all he could to the game. He earned college scholarships to Jefferson College (Hillsboro, Mo.) and Missouri Baptist College (St. Louis). After a career-ending shoulder injury during his junior year, Joshua joined the real world.

Joshua has a daughter and a son who are such incredible people; they brighten his days with laughter, support, and love for one another. Joshua resides in Lake St. Louis, where he spends time with his children studying leadership and character principles. Joshua has studied material on these subjects from authors such as Mack Story, Ria Story, and Stephen R. Covey.

Joshua still enjoys healthy competition and seeks excellence in everything he does.

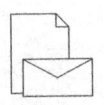

Chad Smith

Finishing Strong

The course of life can be viewed as a race. Sometimes, it will be a sprint. At others, it will be a slow walk … step by step … where hurdles and barriers impede our progression.

I liken it to my experience as a track athlete in junior high. Coach Johnson introduced us to a variety of events, but being a former college pole vaulter, his enthusiasm was evident for that event. Coach encouraged the many athletes who had an interest to meet him at the pole vault pit on the mezzanine of the gym. After getting all the tips and tricks, it was my turn on the runway. The pole seemed heavier than I imagined. I got up to sprinting speed and placed the pole into the box, but barely got off the ground as I flew into the cushioned pit. This might be harder than it looks.

After a few trials, I was getting higher each time. On the next run, I went as hard as I could and was so focused on going up that my momentum was not carried into the pit. Instead, I reached a barrier and helplessly fell backward onto the concrete floor. That, right there, closed my career in pole vaulting but opened my eyes to the various challenges life may bring.

I faced similar obstacles running hurdles as a freshman. I had watched Olympic hurdlers but trying it myself was quite different. The hurdles seemed *so* tall. In fact, it was consistently difficult to get over the hurdles used in the 100-meter dash, and I quickly decided that focusing on the 300-meter intermediate hurdles would be better for my stature and leg length. Fast forward to live competition. I left the blocks and kept pace. Through the first several hurdles, it was easy to keep decent form. As I strived to keep up in the home stretch, it became more about simply getting over the hurdle than having proper form. I still had the opportunity to finish respectably, but then, the unthinkable: I hit the second-to-last hurdle and went down. Embarrassingly, I got up and stepped over the last hurdle before hustling to the finish line. All these years later, that experience is a vivid representation of what we may face in life and offers the type of wisdom a father can impart to his children. The thrill of victory, and the agony of defeat.

We place a high value on perfection. As a child watching ABC's "Wide World of Sports," I would hear Jim McKay: "The thrill of victory, and the agony of defeat." Yet, I've learned that the opportunities for perfection or finishing first are truly rare. Regrettably, there were only isolated times I shared that sentiment with my children. Ella, my youngest daughter, was the last one eligible for Upward Basketball. Despite it being "rec league" competition with a focus on promoting the discovery of Jesus, my other goal as a coach was to win. Early season practices were fun but challenging. Getting the team to master the skills and drills was not going well. After losing the first couple of games, frustration was on their faces and some lost their will to compete. If the goal was perfection, we were failing.

I learned a lot about myself and what motivates kids. We continued to lose throughout the regular season and in Ella's words, "My team is terrible!" Despite this, they battled hard, and soon, the discouragement of losing was overcome by their celebrations for the improvement they were making and for the friendships they were developing.

Our game plan mirrored the focus of Upward. The players needed encouragement and to know they were loved no matter the score. They needed the kind of unconditional love and support that Jesus gives to everyone. A silver lining did appear during that season. We played our last tournament game as the lowest seed but came out as if we were champions — determination, teamwork, and lots of laughter were the reasons we won. We ended the season as victors. The grownup Ella reminds me the other team was missing its best player. I prefer to think it was motivation that fueled the win!

It is hard to imagine overcoming an impassible barrier, yet my youngest son, Dylan, faced this at 19. His identity and passion were focused on playing college football, and he chose Central College in Pella, Iowa, primarily for this reason. The fall football season of 2020 was canceled due to the pandemic, though he was eager to hit the field for the spring season. We talked about once a week, getting an update on his schoolwork; however, we mostly discussed football and his workouts. After the second week of spring practices, he was excited to tell us about moving up to first-team defensive back. Just a few days later, he tore the ACL in his left knee, putting an end to those dreams. It was his third injury resulting in surgery over three years. Prior to that, he had silently decided to stop playing if he got seriously hurt again.

There are many times when God says "yes" to our requests; there are others when the answer is "no." It is then that when we may realize His grace is sufficient and part of His grander plan for our life. Faced with this barrier, Dylan decided to attend college closer to home, grew a deeper relationship with his siblings, started a lawn care business, and studied overseas in Malta for a semester. Dylan is grateful for a greater plan that is being played out in his life.

How we respond to hurdles and barriers defines where we place our hope and possibly the integrity of our faith. My two oldest children, Jessica and Colin, faced circumstances that defined them and their paths forward. When asked what helped her, Jessica told me that in her journaling she began to ask God to break her heart for what breaks His heart. Soon, she would begin serving in a women's prison ministry. This challenged her worldview and shaped the woman she is today. She served women whose life circumstances and emotional trauma were overwhelming. Their response resulted in imprisonment, yet they, too, would be given another chance and ultimately be defined by where they placed their hope and the integrity of their faith. Serving others helped alleviate the burden of Jessica's circumstances and gave her hope!

Colin faced a challenge early in his adult life that brought pause to his pursuits and refined his vision. He was excited to be accepted to medical school though sobered at the overwhelming financial cost to attend. I faced the same situation nearly 26 years prior and pursued a scholarship through the U.S. Navy that covered the entire cost in exchange for a military service contract. He pursued a similar scholarship and believed his chances for selection were excellent. His recruiting officer felt so as well. Upon learning he did not get selected, five months before medical school would begin, Colin was at an impasse. He later told me, "It caused me to reconsider everything that I was doing and why I was doing it."

Ultimately, he would enter medical school, arranging for exorbitant loans and recognizing he would be in debt for many years. During orientation week, Colin attended a student fair highlighting available opportunities for support. Armed forces representatives were there, and he recognized his previous recruiter. Colin talked with him about whether an abbreviated scholarship may still be an option.

The recruiter again expressed his dismay and postulated that Colin's Medical College Acceptance Test (MCAT) score must have been the reason. Colin had retaken his exam and improved his score significantly; unfortunately, the recruiter had submitted a lower previous score with his application. Upon learning of this mistake, the recruiter contacted the selection personnel for reconsideration. By divine provision, there had been some students who had not accepted their scholarship, allowing for Colin's selection and fully financing his medical school costs. The pause and struggle focused Colin's purpose and commitment, preparing him for the blessing to come.

Reflection on our path through life can provide great hope. For most, it will not be executing the perfect race, basking in the celebration of the crowd, or receiving a gold medal. It will more likely be a walk, stopping and starting as we navigate barriers and hurdles. I had felt this way in March 2003 while deployed with the U.S. Navy in support of Operation Iraqi Freedom. My role with Charlie Surgical Company placed me just outside of Nasiriyah, Iraq. In the early stages of the war, there was uncertainty, news of difficult progress, and the capture of U.S. forces in Nasiriyah. During a sandstorm, a U.S. Marine opened the flap to our tent and alerted us that the perimeter had been breached and we were to put our weapon at ready condition. As a medical officer, we carried 9mm guns in the war zone. Mine was covered in sand so I attempted to clean it out. This was an impossible task as the sand in the air filled the barrel as fast as I could clean it.

Exhausted from the completion of my shift and the stress of the circumstances, I holstered the gun and put it away. If I were put in a position to die, this gun filled with sand would not be my savior. I pulled out my Bible and turned to Psalms 23. The words read: "The Lord is my shepherd; I shall not want. He makes me to lie down in green pastures. He leads me beside still waters. He restores my soul. He leads me in paths of righteousness for his name's sake. Even though I walk through the valley of the shadow of death, I will fear no evil, for you are with me …"

I eventually drifted off to sleep and awakened the next morning to learn the perimeter breach was friendly U.S. forces who were off target due to the confusion caused by the sandstorm. Much like this life, this had been a hurdle to progressing to a better day.

Chad Smith | Finishing Strong

Chad Smith was raised in Oak Grove, Mo., as a middle child. His father was an excavator, and his mother managed the household while working in accounting and information technology. Growing up, he learned the value of hard work; his mother shared the gospel of Christ, laying the foundation of his faith.

Chad graduated from Truman State University in Kirksville, Mo., with a degree in biology, followed by medical school at Des Moines University in Iowa on a Navy scholarship. He graduated with a doctor's degree in osteopathic medicine and entered residency training at Naval Hospital Camp Pendleton, Calif., where he served as chief resident. Chad completed seven years of active-duty service, including deployments in Japan and the Middle East. He has served the Warrenton, Mo., community as a family physician for the past 20 years.

He met his wife, Tracy, in college. They married in 1994 and are blessed with four children. Chad and Tracy own a quaint Long Row Lavender flower farm and café in the Midwest.

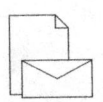

Henrique Friosi

Fatherhood Overcoming Challenges

The Discovery

It was a Thursday morning and, as usual, I was attending a daily operations meeting when my phone rang. To my surprise, it was my ex-girlfriend calling. We had broken up the previous weekend.

"Henrique, I need to talk to you. I *think* I'm pregnant."

At that moment, I lost my breath for a few seconds until I could ask, "But why do you think that? Did you take a test?"

She replied, "Yes."

I followed up: "Did you take a pharmacy test or a blood test?"

She said, "Blood test."

My reaction was, "Well, you don't *think* you're pregnant then; you really *are* pregnant!"

I was not prepared for this. Who is? It wasn't in my plans to become a father at that moment. I had other plans, and I didn't know what to do. I was afraid of how everything would unfold from then on.

The following months were spent trying to fix some things in my head and my heart. It's in moments like these that we can truly see who will stand by our side and who won't. At that time, we weren't sure about the future of our relationship, and with that, I could see both sides. While my parents supported me, encouraging that everything would be OK, my ex's parents blamed me. They said I didn't care about family, was only focused on work and money, and that I didn't need to worry about my child because they would take care of him. Some friends excluded me from invitations, especially one whom I considered my best friend, but he chose to please his wife, taking her side.

Today, more than five years later, I can conclude that no one is ready for a situation such as this. There is no course, preparatory training, or college that teaches you how to deal with such life situations. That's why it's important to be prepared for what is expected while preparing for the unexpected.

The Birth

Always somewhat anxious, Henri was born a few weeks earlier than expected. As a father, the feeling of holding him for only a few seconds and knowing he would need to go to the ICU because he was born underweight and still needed to strengthen his lungs made me scared, even numb. Days went by during visiting hours at the hospital, with some days full of good news about progress, others of agony, being able to see him only through glass, unable to hold him. The only thing I remember from those days is the journey between the hospital and home. It seemed like the world was standing still. I have no memories of those days beyond traffic, the waiting room, and the incubator.

Finally, there was a day when I could finally hold him. I remember picking him up, agitated, straight from the incubator, and laying him on my chest with his head on my left shoulder. After a few minutes, he calmed down and stayed that way until he fell asleep. Even today, more than five years later, this is one of the most effective ways to calm him down and make him sleep. And it works only with me.

The New Family Relationship

Perhaps one of the few pieces of advice I could give to parents in a situation like mine: Solve your problems with the mother of your children. If you want to be part of your child's life and positively affect his or her life, you need to do this; you are responsible for it. Marcos Piangers, a Brazilian writer who is famous for sharing his insights on fatherhood, says something very interesting about raising children when there is a separation: "Each one is fighting with the only weapons they have; the man does not want to give money to the woman, and the woman does not want to let the man see the children. The resentment each has for the other makes each use the sword they have." In the end, who loses?

It does not matter what happened or who was to blame for the breakup. What matters is fixing the relationship, and that's what you as a father and a man should do. That's what real men do — they solve the situation when it's not easy. I can say that when a separated father starts a new relationship, the relationship that was already somewhat harmonious can regress again. I see many men who are separated fathers who, when they start a new relationship, end up distancing themselves from their children, and unfortunately, many times this is influenced by the new girlfriend.

I remember one of the first conversations I had with Leticia, the first woman I dated after Henri was born, who ended up becoming my wife. It was about what she thought about being in a relationship with someone who already had a child. At that moment, we aligned that he was and would always be my priority. I can't understand how there can be fathers who distance themselves from their children because of other relationships. At the end of the day, the one who will lose the most with this is the father himself. I understand this alignment was fundamental to setting expectations and making many decisions.

There, however, was the other side of this connection, which was the relationship of this person who was now with me, my son and his mother, Ana. From the first months of our relationship, I made sure Leticia had contact with Henri, but the relationship between the two women was still somewhat troubled. From Ana's side, there was the fear of a new woman being with her son, not knowing how she would treat him and considering the vast number of depictions of stepmothers in animated movies, her fears were warranted. On the part of Leticia, there was uncertainty about how to deal with the whole situation. So, the relationship unfolded in the early years with meetings where no one felt comfortable, both greeting each other out of obligation and interacting as little as possible. Until one day, this needed to change.

It was December 2021, and as usual, Henri was spending the end of the year with us. At that moment, Leticia and I were living in the Brazilian city of Uberlandia, MG, which is 1,000 kilometers from Primavera do Leste, MT, the city where Henri and his mother lived. That day, Henri started feeling unwell; he has asthma, so we were very attentive not to let a crisis evolve. He started having a high fever in the evening, a severe cough, refused to eat anything, and began to show a lot of weakness. Whenever things like this happen, I normally stay in direct contact with Ana to understand the treatments he undergoes. This time, we decided to take him to the hospital for a more detailed evaluation by a pediatrician. It was around 8:00 or 9:00 p.m., and the three of us were heading to the hospital.

We arrived, went through triage, and waited for the attendance. Then, my phone battery died, and I stopped communicating with Ana. Sometime later, when Henri was already being attended to and medicated (luckily, it wasn't anything serious), my wife asked if she should send a message to Ana because she must be worried. Well, in my head, I thought there was a chance she wouldn't respond, but at least she would be informed of what was happening and that everything was fine.

It's moments like these when things happen and we can't explain them. After that day, the relationship between the two transformed. The ice that existed was broken. Ana could see in detail the care that Leticia was giving to Henri and that she could indeed be a good stepmother to him. Funny enough, nowadays there are times when the two are talking and exchanging photos of Henri, photos that I don't even receive.

Of all the things I've done in my life — so many successful projects, achieved goals, fulfilled dreams — perhaps building this family relationship is what I can say is my greatest success. I am sure that, in the future, Henri will be grateful for this achievement.

Redefining "Manhood"

Final thoughts: After becoming a father, I started listening to many podcasts and reading some books trying to seek knowledge on the subjects of fatherhood, masculinity, and the role men play in society. Learning how men behave today has left me uncomfortable. I do not exclude myself from this environment; I have had and still have some similar behaviors that don't make me proud. Today, there is a celebrant of the immature man: the macho man who drinks the most alcohol, the one who gets the most women, the one who shares sophomoric viewpoints of women in their groups. There are some men who always feel the need to prove to their circle of friends that he is the most manly.

A real man is born masculine; he doesn't have to prove that he is macho. The role of a real man is to protect his tribe, provide security for his family, and develop his surroundings. Unfortunately, or fortunately, when we understand that this is our role and make the choice to follow it, many "friendships" can be left behind. Many will judge your choices, others will mock them, and some will even criticize, saying it is best to do the complete opposite. I have learned to just let go and focus on the purpose.

My purpose is to try to be the best example for my son, and so far, he has helped me overcome some problems. One, as simple as it may seem, is that he helps me say, "I love you." For some reason, saying those words to people I love is not something I can naturally do. During my life, I have not heard this from many men. I have unconsciously internalized the stereotype that men should not say, "I love you." Let's try to break that. Love you all!

Henrique Friosi | Fatherhood Overcoming Challenges

Henrique Friosi was born and raised in Brazil, having lived in several cities throughout several regions of the country. After graduating in industrial engineering with an MBA in business management, Henrique joined one of the world's largest agribusiness companies in 2012 as an intern and progressed his career in positions of operational excellence and innovation. Like his parents, he moved several times to assume new positions.

In 2018, Henrique's son, Henri, was born. Despite living far apart since birth, it has never prevented them from being close, whether through a 1,200-mile car trip to spend the weekend together or an international flight to pick him up for Christmas in the U.S. and see snow for the first time.

Henrique has lived in St. Louis with his wife, Leticia, since 2022. He spends his free time traveling back and forth to see Henri and undergoing triathlon training for his first Ironman competition.

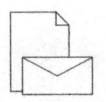

Willie Blue

I Survived It

I was trying to recall fond memories of my father; I couldn't think of anything. I can remember when I first started to hate him. It was on my 13th birthday. He showed no interest and didn't even remember it was my birthday. I tried to rationalize by saying he had too many children to remember everybody. He did more for my older brother than he ever did for me. I think he liked him more. After I left home, he became closer to my youngest brother. My youngest brother used to pick him up from work. My brother told me he would introduce him to his friends and coworkers.

After thinking about it for a while, I realized the one thing that still sticks in my mind is that he tried to kill me once. I think it was when I was around six years old, and he put a rope around my neck and dragged me across the floor, and one of his friends stopped him. I don't know why that wasn't one of the things that made me start to hate him. I think I used transference during that time. I placed the blame on my father's friend rather than on him.

My father was an alcoholic, and he was very abusive physically and emotionally. There was a thing we had to do once he came home early from work on Friday evenings. We could approach him and hug him, but if he came home late, we had to stay out of his way because it meant he had been out drinking. He would hit us for no reason at all. Sometimes, he would even punch us. Not only was he an alcoholic, he was a womanizer as well. The one reason I think he didn't like me was he was making passes at a lady in the store, and the store owner asked him, "Don't you think the child will tell his mother what you are doing?" I'm sure I didn't tell her because I didn't know what was happening.

The one thing that has stayed with me my whole life was a statement my father used to say about me that I was worthless, good for nothing, and would never amount to anything—those words stuck with me, even to this day. I sometimes still feel the sting. Whenever I fail at something or don't complete a task, I sometimes think about those words. When you look back over my life, I know I'm not worthless, good-for-nothing, and will never amount to anything. If I had to compare my life to his, I served 24 years in the United States Army; he only served six. He had a sixth-grade education; I have an associate's degree, a bachelor's degree, and a dual master's degree. He had us living in houses that should have been condemned; I have lived in two houses I had built. In all fairness, I don't think I should compare because we lived in two different periods. He had to struggle to survive. I struggled for a while, but now, I'm thriving. When I started my family, I wanted them to have the best I could give them.

I came close to killing my father once. It was the time I stood up and didn't back down. He was very angry and started toward me. I did not look away. I looked him straight in the eyes and didn't budge. I think this surprised him and probably scared him, as well, because he stopped about a foot from what I call the kill zone. I had a knife down by my side where he couldn't see it. I knew where I would hit him first, which would've startled him enough that I could've completed the job. I'm so glad he didn't come any closer, so I didn't do what I had planned. I would've gone to jail and messed up my opportunity to prove him wrong.

When I became a stronger Christian, I also realized my wrongs. I had to forgive him and ask him to forgive me for whatever I had done that caused him to feel the way he did about me. The day came, but it was too late. He had dementia and didn't know who I was. I also felt sad for him and me because I would not get a chance to hear his response. I had to forgive him in absentia and ask God to forgive me on my father's behalf. Years later, at my father's funeral, I realized I wasn't over it. One of our cousins got up to make remarks. My cousin spoke about what a remarkable man my father was and how he helped this single mom by buying groceries for her and the kids. It dawned on me that we were trying to survive on the little food he would leave there for us. People used to tell me that maybe he didn't know how to love, and the times were hard back then. My comeback on that is if he had love and compassion for someone else outside of the house, then what about his family? I think the family should come first, and then whatever you have left over, if possible, if you talk it over with your family, you can share it with others.

He may have had too many children to be able to love them all. I only have one son, and I wish I had more children to prove wrong the theory that he had too many children to love. I love my son dearly, and I wish we had more time together. His mother took him away from me when he was 2 years old. I thought it would only be for a short while so she could help her mother set up a wilderness store. It turns out that was an excuse she used to get away from me. That's another very long story that's too long to tell at this time. I got to visit with them when he was four years old. It wasn't a very good visit because I found out that my wife wanted to make the separation permanent. Looking back on it, I wish I had taken custody of my son, but I was in the military and didn't have any support near me to help me take care of him.

We would visit from time to time. He would visit me, and I would visit him. Then, after a while, we had a 14-year break, and I didn't understand why. I found out I had a granddaughter who was three years old. We finally got together, and I saw my granddaughter for the first time when she was 6. I only got to spend three hours with her because she was getting ready to go on a vacation with her mother. At this writing, she is 13. I hope to spend quality time with them in July of this year. I love my son and try to tell him and my granddaughter as often as possible. My father never told me that he loved me. I think I told my father when I saw him with dementia. I never reconciled with my father, but I did with my son. We hugged and kissed and told each other we loved each other. Things seem to be better with us. I'll update you on how it went in my future book.

If my father could somehow read this from wherever he is in the hereafter, I want him to know that I became a better man than he thought I would. I'm stronger and more resilient, thriving, and continuing to believe in God. Maybe his negativity pushed me to a more positive outcome.

My note to present-day fathers and future fathers is to always love your children. Teach your children to love themselves. Teach them to dream and dream big. Don't just tell your children you love them. Show them. Spend quality time as a family. Get to know each child individually, and for God's sake, don't pick favorites. They will be able to see it. Help them to cultivate whatever dreams or ideas they may have. Never put them down, calling them stupid or lazy, or any negative labels that you can place on them. Don't be too big to forgive them when they or you make a mistake.

Willie Blue is retired and lives in St. Charles, Mo. He has served 24 years in the United States Army, ten years in state government, and seven years in real estate. He is starting one of his lifelong dreams of becoming a writer. Willie is an award-winning speaker and a 24-year member of Toastmasters International, a nonprofit educational organization that teaches public speaking skills. Willie is also a member of the National Speakers Association St. Louis Chapter. Willie believes you're never too old to pursue your dreams.

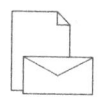

Mike Forness

A Dad's Gift

The following is from a letter I wrote to each of my children as they started their Senior year of High School, revised for this note.. While the following words were originally meant for my children, I want to share them with you, too. Maybe you grew up without a dad in your life. Perhaps you're still in a home without a father figure or positive male role model to help you navigate childhood and prepare you for life as an adult. If that's the case, I believe you're reading this chapter. It is not an accident but rather divine intervention from your Father in heaven, who loves you immeasurably more than any earthly father ever could.

If you're reading this book and you've found your way to this chapter, keep reading. I hope that you find these words to be an encouragement and that they provide you with hope for a future as the best version of yourself that you can be...that you want to be. Most importantly, I hope that if you don't know Jesus Christ as your personal Lord and Savior, you come to know Him personally because He and God love you unconditionally.

Today marks a significant milestone as you embark on your senior year of high school. This new chapter in your life is one that we have shared closely, and as your father, I want to offer you guidance that has shaped my own journey in the hope that it will enrich yours.

First and foremost, put Jesus Christ at the center of your life. There is a space within each of us that only He can fill. By keeping faith at the forefront, you will find strength and guidance in every aspect of life. Just as you strive to be the first one to the line on the athletic field, carry this leadership into every area of your life. You will encounter challenges where you might feel outmatched in speed, size, or skill, but with unwavering determination and hard work, you can overcome any obstacle.

Surround yourself with people who uplift you. Choose friends and teammates who challenge you to improve and support you when you falter. Be that friend and teammate to others as well—someone who gives more than you expect in return, someone who shares your strengths to enhance the group. Remember, the happiness and respect you receive are direct reflections of what you contribute to the lives of others.

Believe in yourself. My very first priority was to teach you to believe in yourself. You have all the abilities you will ever need to be a champion. You have the capacity to learn; you put in the time and effort, and it shows in your performance. The most important thing you can do now is to believe in yourself. Believe in yourself, and you can achieve your goals, no matter how outlandish they may seem or how far out of reach they may look. If you first believe in yourself, then nothing is out of reach. Know that you can accomplish more working together and trusting in your team than you can alone. Never sacrifice your values for victory.

Be a role model. The world needs more individuals who lead not only by their words but through their actions. Foster a legacy that prioritizes values over mere achievements. Embrace lifelong learning. Learn something new every day – not just the *"what,"* but the *"why,"* the *"how,"* and the *"what else."* Be a critical thinker that asks questions. Don't just memorize the quote, but learn the author's context and the whole message. Don't just accept the opinion, but learn the pros and cons, the facts for and against that opinion. Understand the deeper reasons behind facts and figures and the broader context of knowledge you gain. This approach will build your confidence and nurture a spirit of humility. Knowledge and ability breeds confidence, and emotional intelligence breeds humility. So be smart and humble because you are able to do so.

Be your own best advocate. Voice your thoughts and stand up, not only for yourself but also for others. Your influence can make a positive contribution to society and help shape the community around you. Remember, the environment you live in is not just inherited; it is also shaped by your actions and decisions.

As you step forward, you must define what success means to you. You already have the tools to be successful. From this point forward in your journey, it is your responsibility to decide how you will define success. As your dad, let me try to influence your definition of success by telling you what success is *not*. Success is something other than your athletic accomplishments, high school, college, or career accomplishments. Success is *not* a title, a career, a car, or a house. True success is *not* about visible achievements; instead, it is the sum of your impact on others and the legacy of your character — the sum of your life's work as others recall your presence. It is the impression you make on others when you leave the room, your impact on someone else's success, and how they define their success. So reach for the stars, enjoy the journey, and never avoid giving back. Cherish each step of your journey, and always look for ways to contribute positively to the world around you.

Unfortunately, along with successes, you will inevitably face losses. As much as I wish I could shield you from them, experiencing defeat is a part of life. What matters is that you get back up and continue to strive forward, learning from each setback and appreciating the moments you have. My biggest regret is probably shared by every parent, and it is that

I can prepare you to win, but I can't protect you from loss. It will happen; you will lose games, friends, jobs, and other things throughout life. But you must continue to play, continue to compete, and appreciate the time you have. My investment in you is to provide you with the tools to succeed and make good decisions, and then pray that you will only experience joy, knowing I played a small part in making you strong enough to overcome anything.

Throughout your life, you will meet mentors, each with something new to teach you. You will have different coaches, teachers, and leaders in your life. We need diversity of thought for growth. They will have different teaching methods, tactics, and levels of connection with you. Don't discount anyone new just because they are new. Understand that you can learn something from everyone. Remain true to your goals and take advantage of the knowledge they provide. Embrace the diversity in thought and approach they bring. Every lesson enriches your understanding and contributes to your growth.

Reflecting on our time together, I am filled with gratitude for the memories we've created. From the struggles that ended in breakthroughs to the triumphs that exceeded your expectations, each moment has been a stepping stone in your development. You have given me a gift. It is demonstrated in the simplest of acts. I will remember your frustrated looks until it clicked for you. I will remember the first time you did something you didn't think was possible. I remember the day you decided that you deserved to win and the day that second place wasn't good enough. I have so many memories, and they have all added to the person I am today.

Finally, always know that I love you. My love for you is boundless. I take immense pride in what you have achieved and in the person you are becoming. We will always be close. We will always share a deep connection because part of me lives on through you, in every challenge you meet and in every dream you realize. My gift to you is a small part of me that I would gladly give again and again.

I love you. I am proud of you.

Dad

NOTES FROM DAD

Mike Forness, originally from Tulsa, Oklahoma, and a resident of St. Louis since 1999, is a dedicated father of four, with three of his children currently in college and one in junior high. Deeply rooted in his Christian faith, Mike values the importance of relationships and service to others, striving to nurture strong connections with family and friends. He has built a successful career in technology sales over the past two decades, showcasing his commitment and expertise. An alumnus of Oklahoma State University, Mike is an ardent Cowboys fan, an enthusiastic outdoorsman, and passionate about fitness. He is actively involved in F3, a community for men that combines physical fitness with the development of leadership skills, reflecting his commitment to personal growth and community engagement.

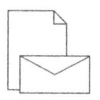

Kyle Veltrop

Pain, Triumph and Joy

Among the countless photos of my three sons growing up, there are a few that stand out. None are staged, just instinctively captured in the moment. There's one of them on a beach in Alabama, standing side by side, staring at the Gulf of Mexico as the sun goes down. There's one of them in a pumpkin patch with an autumnal hue in the air.

Then there's my favorite: The three of them walking the track after a middle school football game. Eli, my oldest, is on crutches with a broken leg, sustained at a high school football practice. In the middle is my middle, Owen, fresh off a standout performance at quarterback to lead his team to victory. To his right is a young Ty, wearing a Pittsburgh Steelers jersey, happily lugging Owen's helmet and shoulder pads. The three are talking, laughing. This picture resonates because, in one snapshot, it represents what sports have meant to me as a dad: some pain, plenty of triumph and a hell of a lot of joy.

The Passion

Growing up, I played team sports but what I remember more are the marathon backyard sessions of Wiffle ball, touch football or pickup basketball games with my brother and neighborhood friends. I collected baseball cards and plastic batting helmets. At night, I'd lay on the floor next to our Buick-sized radio and listen to St. Louis Cardinals baseball games. I devoured the sports section in the newspaper. I spent the last two years at the University of Missouri keeping stats at football and basketball games from the press box or press row. I spent the first 15 years of my career working as a sportswriter/editor.

My sons had no choice but to live in a sports-soaked world. Not that they ever fought it. Football, basketball, baseball, they have played them all. I coached their youth teams. They spent their nights and weekends practicing and playing, playing and practicing. When they had downtime, they'd gather around the TV and watch games.

Our sports journey together has led to so many memories, so many life experiences.

The Pain

Aside from Eli's broken leg, he broke his collarbone in a middle school football game. He missed a couple of games as a senior after spraining his knee. Then, toward the end of Eli's senior season, while working at a restaurant, he had a glass shatter in his hand, severely cutting tendons. Surgery was required; he would miss Senior Night.

Owen's injuries were even more scarring, literally. Owen took over the starting quarterback job as a sophomore in high school. He threw a beautiful deep ball, was a tough runner. But on the final drive of the final game of his junior season, Owen tore his right ACL. That injury cost him that season of basketball, his second love, and signed him up for a strenuous, grueling rehabilitation. He tackled it like it was a ballcarrier in the open field.

Owen pushed himself hard in physical therapy sessions. He spent so much time with the high school trainer that the two became frequent texting buddies. I got an email from an assistant coach telling me how amazed he was that Owen never missed an offseason workout, even though he couldn't do much at all. Instead of curling up, he stood tall.

On the spring day he got fully cleared for all physical activity, he texted Eli and me with this overjoyed message, "Let's goooooooo!" Owen then went to work. He organized throwing sessions with his receivers. He trained with quarterback coaches at a local performance academy. Owen attended a college scouting combine. He looked great during 7-on-7 tournaments during that summer. He was ready for his senior season.

On the first drive of his first game, Owen ran around the corner of the line, juked the opposing star player — a Mizzou recruit — and then crumpled, untouched, to the ground. And he didn't get up. I uttered an expletive, audible to those around me. Owen had torn his left ACL.

After the team's postgame huddle in the end zone, players and coaches hugged Owen before boarding the team bus. Even two opposing coaches walked over to tell him how crestfallen they were to see him go down. Owen stayed strong, but after I helped him up the stairs, he turned and collapsed in my arms, sobbing.

There were other challenges. Eli and Owen's high school football team has long struggled, and it reached a nadir during Eli's senior season. During one game, we lost to injury three players to an already undersized and undermanned offensive line. With the score already lopsided, the head coaches met at halftime and our coach said he thought it'd be best to not finish the game.

Eli made a detour on the way to the locker room and found his family on the track in front of the visitor's stands. He clutched me hard, burying his facemask into my collarbone (three days later, I still had small bruises). He'd say later: "I can stand losing 42-6; I'm used to that. But to quit …"

The head coach resigned shortly after. The school's principal and athletic director met with the team and told the players it was perfectly fine if they didn't want to finish the season. Eli and a fellow senior captain bristled. They vowed to show their school, their families and other teams that the bond the team had created wasn't breakable. It wasn't a locker room of quitters.

Eli and Owen's high school football careers were filled with loads of adversity, but they came out stronger for it. They had teammates over for Monday Night Football games, gave players rides to and from practice, hosted team meals, regularly opened our home to some of the guys who lived in St. Louis city so they could more easily attend practices and team functions.

At the season-end banquet, as president of the booster club, I addressed the team, with this message: "You guys suited up, showed up, gave it your all. That's half of life, brothers."

Even if you lose a lot of games, that doesn't make you a loser.

The Triumph

Eli started as a freshman on both the varsity football and baseball teams. He made acrobatic catches as a wide receiver and was a big-hitting center fielder. He played for one of the top travel summer high school baseball teams.

Owen was always the top pitcher on his youth baseball teams. He was a sweet shooter in basketball with a complete all-around game. He received all-conference recognition in football at both quarterback and safety.

Ty mauled the ball and blew fastballs past hitters during his time playing baseball. In basketball, he is a strong passer, ballhandler, rebounder and defender. And there's football, his biggest love. He excels on the offensive and defensive lines, and as an eighth-grader played for a high-level select team that won the league championship. His coaches raved not just about his performance but his approach. Ty's football future is bright.

There are challenges that come with being a sports dad. There are jam-packed schedules; long days in the bleachers; a lot of hard pretzels, gooey nachos and shriveled hot dogs from the concession stand. Sports participation can be expensive.

The rewards, however, have far outweighed those challenges, and not just from watching my sons find success in their playing arenas. There have been conversations in the car, lasting friendships forged, team meals, sharing lessons that also apply to life — control what you can control, be coachable and a good teammate, be consistent in your approach each and every day.

The Joy

On the day of Eli's last high school football game, he sent the following text to my wife and me: "before tonight, i just wanna thank you guys for everything you've done regarding football. thank you for driving me to youth football practice every day, thank you for sitting through the hot, the cold, and the rain just to watch me play. ... and thank you guys for always being my biggest fans. i love you both and appreciate you more than words can describe."

That night, just days after the surgery on his hand and while wearing a large cast, Eli caught a touchdown pass. The pass came from his brother.

The first game of the following season, Owen's junior year, he engineered an upset win of a rival high school, throwing and running for touchdowns. On the bus ride home, he sent me this text: "That one was for you."

Even now, with Eli and Owen in college and their playing days but memories, sports continue to bind our family. I welled up when Owen drove in from college and walked into Ty's playoff football game to surprise him on his birthday. I share a fantasy football team with Owen and Ty. The four of us have a group text that often revolves around sports. We get together to watch games and eat good food. We always have a connection for a conversation.

I prominently display pictures of games I went to with each: Eli at a St. Louis Cardinals game, Owen at an LSU football game in Baton Rouge, Ty at Fenway Park in Boston. And there's the four of us together in front of the Superdome before a New Orleans Saints game.

Those pictures are cherished, but they aren't my favorite. No, that's the one after a middle school football game, the one that shows three boys depicting some pain, a lot of triumph and a hell of a lot of joy.

Just like life.

NOTES FROM DAD

Kyle Veltrop was born and raised in Jefferson City, Mo., the youngest of six children. His father, a World War II veteran, was an accomplished cattle farmer who instilled in his family the value of hard work and being part of the community. Kyle's mom held their home together and has been his biggest supporter. A native of New Orleans, she also taught Kyle to love cooking and good food.

Kyle graduated from the University of Missouri with a Bachelor of Journalism degree. St. Louis has been home since 1992. His career highlight is working for 14 years as an editor and feature writer for *The Sporting News*, where he covered Major League Baseball, nine men's basketball NCAA Tournaments and the Super Bowl. Kyle now works as a freelance journalist, where among his roles included working with the authors on their chapters as the writing coach and editor for "Notes From Dad."

Kyle married Shannon in 1996. They have three sons who are in graduate school, college and high school.

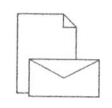

Dan Luigs

The Road Less Traveled: A Father-Daughter Journey

Dad: I'm glad we are headed to go hiking together, just you and me. The weather couldn't be better! One more hour and we'll be there.

Daughter: Dad, I've got a question. Why do you buy us gloves, bats, and coaching and help us so much with sports?

Dad: Great question. I want you to excel in whatever you are passionate about, sports or life in general. I see how much you like playing softball and are a good player. People learn so much faster when they have a great coach and when you spend time with people that are better than you.

Daughter: That makes sense. Thank you.

Dad: As I think about it more, I realize I didn't have these advantages as a kid. I wanted to be a great baseball player but didn't know what to do or what it would take to be great. I knew I needed help. As an adult, I was able to find and connect with people who helped me succeed.

Daughter: What kind of help did you get?

Dad: Help with business, fitness, faith, loving your mom, being a better dad, and becoming the man I always wanted to be.

Daughter: Did you say you got help being a better dad?

Dad: (laughs) I sure did. It's funny; they say the teacher appears when the student is ready. Some of my friends introduced me to a guy who was writing a book about being a good dad around the time you were born. Being a good dad was something I wanted to be. I wanted to be around someone who spent time studying, practicing, and teaching others to be a good dad. So, we became friends, and I've learned a lot from him. My friend Brian taught me the importance of studying things that matter, practicing things that matter, and teaching things that matter to others. People learn the best when they teach.

Daughter: Wow. I'm glad you met him. What are some things you learned from him?

Dad: Quite a bit. He has some kids older than you, so I was able to learn from some of the mistakes he made. He's continually learning and sharing what it's like to be a dad to teenagers, and his oldest is getting ready to head to college.

Daughter: I like to make money. Tell me about the business guy.

Dad: People helped me at different stages of my career. The manager at the insurance company where I worked had grown and sold a couple of businesses. He showed me what I needed to get started and was the first person who told me about hiring others to help me accomplish my goals. He told me I couldn't afford to be the one doing a $10-an-hour job when I was a $100-an-hour person.

Daughter: You made $100 an hour to start at that job?

Dad: That's funny. No! I made very little. And it was a major sacrifice to pay someone else. However, leveraging their time allowed me to focus on higher-productive activities that eventually allowed me to make more money. Once time is spent, you can't get it back.

Daughter: You said he helped you get started. Then what happened?

Dad: He had taught me all I knew. So, I prayed a lot about what my next move should be. At church, I met a man who owned an insurance brokerage. And after lots of prayer, learning about him and his business, and asking wise people around me for advice, I decided to join his company. While I was there, I met a great business coach.

Daughter: Did you pay the business coach?

Dad: I did. He wouldn't take payments, so I had to take out a loan.

Daughter: You did what??? You avoid borrowing money. You always tell me to save and invest.

Dad: That's right. I did borrow money, and I invested it in myself. This coach had grown companies and had hired many people to work for him. I wanted to learn how to do that. He believed in me; that gave me confidence.

Daughter: You must believe to achieve!

Dad: Indeed! Do you remember the story in the Bible about the man who buried the talent?

Daughter: Yes

Dad: Well, I never want to be like the man who buried the one talent. You know what happened to him, right?

Daughter: Yes, he was called wicked and slothful. He was cast out into the darkness. I'm not going to waste my talents.

Dad: I'm proud of you. You ask fantastic questions, and that is one of the best skills you can develop. People love to talk and tell stories, and being interested in them will make them like you. Do you know who was great at asking questions?

Daughter: Your mom.

Dad: (laughs) For sure!!! Who else?

Daughter: Jesus asked great questions. People would ask him questions to trap him, and he would use questions back to them, and he escaped their traps.

Dad: Yes! Jesus asked quality questions. He was curious about others and often asked "how" or "why" questions. He almost never asked yes or no questions; his questions were almost always open-ended. His questions were often challenging and caused people to think.

Daughter: I love his question, "Why do you look at the speck of sawdust in your brother's eye and pay no attention to the plank in your own eye?" People tend to find fault in others and blame others for things going wrong. It's important to recognize when we have made a mistake.

Dad: What a great lesson to learn so early in life! When you are playing softball and you make an error, what would you hope your teammates do for you?

Daughter: I hope they cheer me on, tell me that I can do it, and give me a hug if it's really bad.

Dad: You do have some great teammates. Jesus gave people a lot of grace and forgave many. It took me a long time to learn how to forgive, but it's so freeing when you do. Forgiving is a great gift to yourself!!!

Daughter: That sounds like a great podcast topic, Dad. What have you learned from people you have interviewed on your podcast?

Dad: Funny you ask; we might not be on this trip if I hadn't learned about the importance of spending one-on-one time with your kids and your wife from that dad who wrote the book about being a good dad.

Daughter: I know that Dad, don't I?

Dad: Yes, it is Larry, one of my closest friends.

Daughter: What else have you learned from hosting The Journey of a Christian Dad Podcast?

Dad: The last thing I wanted to do was host a podcast. It takes a lot of time, and I'd have to learn something new; I wouldn't be very good at it … but I asked God what he wanted to talk about one night, and he wanted to talk about me starting a Podcast for Christian Dads. So, a BIG thing I learned was to be obedient when God calls you to do something. I resisted at first, but then I trusted God to direct my steps.

Daughter: Was getting the podcast started easy?

Dad: Once I found the right people to help, it became easier. It was the right thing to do. Yes, I had to sacrifice time, and it was difficult. I'm glad I chose the hard road. The hard road often leads to the greatest rewards.

Daughter: What do you know now that you wish you knew when you were my age?

Dad: (takes a deep breath and exhales, slowly holding back tears) When I was a teenager, I didn't feel worthy of God's love, and I didn't feel like I could add much value to others' lives. I wish I knew who I was and that I was worthy of God's love and that people loved me. The more I distanced myself from God, the more ashamed I felt. If the story you are telling yourself doesn't serve you, CHANGE THE STORY!

I changed the story that I was telling myself by saying power statements like:

I AM WORTHY! God made me in the image and likeness of him and He loves me.

I AM WORTHY OF GOD'S LOVE!

I AM WORTHY OF GREAT RELATIONSHIPS!

I AM WORTHY OF SUCCESS!

Every morning, I would scream these power statements. I would pray to God and ask for help becoming the man He wanted me to be. I prayed like everything depended on God and worked like everything depends on me.

My daily habits include writing down things I am grateful for power statements, prayers, and wins. By learning to have an attitude of gratitude and looking for the positive things in life, I have so much more joy and happiness. What you focus on expands.

Daughter: What is your favorite word to focus on?

Dad: *Love* is my favorite word. God is love. And when asked what the greatest commandment is, Jesus said to love the Lord your God with all your heart and with all your soul and with all your mind, and love your neighbor as yourself. One of the big turning points in our life is when we stop seeking the God we want and we start seeking the God who IS.

Sweet girl, I am so glad we are on this journey together!

I LOVE YOU! I BELIEVE IN YOU! I AM PROUD OF YOU!

Daughter: I'll always love you too, Dad! You are always there for me.

P.S. This is a very important life decision. Your choice of a spouse will permanently change your life.

Tips on choosing a spouse:

1. Find one who loves JESUS.

2. Seek wise counsel — Ask people you know about whom you date (parents, teachers, friends, co-workers).

3. Evaluate his parents and their marriage, parenting, values.

4. Compatibility — Do you have similar values and common interests?

Dan Luigs | The Road Less Traveled: A Father-Daughter Journey

Dan Luigs went from a high-income job to no income when starting a business while his wife was pregnant with their first child. He has grown his insurance business, By Referral. into the top 3 percent in the country in less than six years.

Dan's success is based on Zig Ziglar's quote, "You can have everything you want in life, if you will just help other people get what they want."

He is a requested public speaker at Mastermind STL, Realtor Roundtable, St. Charles Association of Realtors, local Chambers of Commerce, and a weekly men's prayer breakfast in Dardenne Prairie. He has been featured on many podcasts including "The Dad Edge Podcast" and "BizDads."

Dan is the founder and host of "The Journey of a Christian Dad Podcast." He also leads a membership community for dads called Dad's Ascent. He loves helping other dads be the leader their family deserves!

Dan and his family love hiking, playing in water, spending time with family and friends, and living a life of abundance!

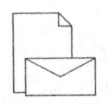

Mike Elam

Growing My Boys!

Being a father is like wading into cool ocean waters on a scorching summer day. There is that initial shock and exhilaration, then you get a bit deeper and find a position where you feel stable, maybe even comfortable. That is when a rogue wave rolls in from behind and smacks you, knocking you off your feet, causing you to struggle to get your head above the water. In truth, that is the everyday feeling of being a parent. Just when you think you have grasped this whole parenting role, life reminds you there is still a lot left to learn. Take, for instance, the time I tried to change my son's diaper, thinking I had it all figured out. Suddenly, he decided it was the perfect moment for a surprise fountain. Lesson learned: Expect the unexpected. Shout out to Big Brother!

I know mothers and daughters share a special bond. I see it between my wife and daughter. There is a special bond with daddies and daughters as well, especially when she is your only daughter, and she is your baby, like mine. It's the feeling that no one will ever truly be worthy of her, and no one will love and protect her like Dad. But my "daddy/daughter" thoughts will have to come later. This chapter is about boys, and the extraordinary bond between a father and son. When I heard those words, "You're going to be a father," life became REAL! But when you have a child, there is a realization you played a role in creating a human being, and the weight and pressure of shaping this new little person's future begins to settle in, as does self-reflection, doubt, and overall freaking out.

Life is a game lived solo, but it is rarely played alone. You are always part of a team. Whether it is a family team, a school team, a work team, a community team, someone is always counting on you to live up to the group's expectations of success. No one counts on you more than your child, especially in those early years. It is the parent-teacher conferences, where you suddenly realize you're part of the school team. You navigate through reports of crayon-eating incidents and finger-painting masterpieces, wondering if you are doing this whole parenting thing right. I remember looking at my newborn son thinking, "I want you to be better than me." So many things I want to share, like the lessons I have learned from my own mistakes, so you can avoid the painful consequences of bad decisions. But I have learned the most through those painful mistakes. Bad decisions become etched in our bones, never to be forgotten. Still, it does not stop my desire to protect and shield my kids from life's pain, while equipping them to become the best version of themselves.

Having a son means carrying on our family name. There is a sense of pride that your branch of the family tree will continue to grow. But with this honor comes a tremendous responsibility — to shape the future chapters of our family's tale in a way that creates a sense of pride. You must take an active role in writing that story.

When I think about the advice I want to impart to my boys, it starts with this: **"Seek wisdom!"** Education is a lifelong pursuit. Whether it is in a classroom or on your own, always strive to learn and improve yourself. Read as much as you can. Solomon was the wisest man who ever lived, so a good place to start is with reading Proverbs, a book filled with advice about the most important things in life. When I took the Gallup Strengths assessment, it talked about how your strengths will always be your strengths, and your weaknesses will always be your weaknesses. While your weaknesses can be strengthened, they will never be a strength. So, spend your efforts building those strengths, and look for ways to offset your weaknesses with those that surround you. Identifying blind spots can keep you from feeling unnecessary pain.

Family comes first. They are the first team you will ever join, so make your membership count. The more you support your family, the more your family will support you. Despite the times they frustrate you, and drive you crazy, they are still your family. You share a bond you will never have with anyone else. Honor that, and do not let it slip away. When your children and grandchildren are connected to extended family, a support system is created allowing everyone to work together. That is a powerful team and one I have seen do amazing things.

Pursue what you love, not what will bring you the most money. Pour your heart and soul into becoming the best at something you genuinely love, and the financial rewards will follow. Chase your dreams no matter what others might tell you! There is natural energy and enthusiasm that only come from living a life dedicated to doing what you love. Life is both precious and fragile. Never take it for granted. Holding back only limits your potential joy. Approach life and love with passion.

Life is hard! **Find a partner to share the load.** But seek a partner who possesses strengths where you are weakest. This will help sharpen you. You will have differences that will require give and take from both. You will challenge each other, which makes you better. In some respects, your spouse knows you better than you know you. I joke, "There is no reason for me to remember my faults. Jennifer tracks them enough for both of us." But in reality, you need someone who will remind you if you are about to repeat a past mistake. A partner holds you accountable and helps you avoid missteps. But to take advantage of this, you have to listen!

The wisest counsel, and the most meaningful conversations, will come from the other side of the bed. When done right, you will face life's battles together and reach heights that would be unattainable alone.

Your word is your most valuable possession; guard it always. If you say something, mean it! There is nothing more painful than disappointing yourself, and you feel that most when you look in the mirror. You can tell others whatever you want, but the face in the mirror knows the truth. Things in life may come and go, but protecting your word and living a life of strong character will endure. Letting others down is painful, but letting yourself down has no escape. Any regrets in life will have this at the center.

Faith is a deeply personal journey and something that adds purpose to your life. It cannot be inherited or chosen for you by someone else. You do not enter heaven's gates because your grandfather was a Southern Baptist minister. The faith decisions you make shape your spiritual destiny. It is an individual choice with eternal consequences. You come in alone and leave alone. Know what your next step will be before you finish here. It is too important to skip. Everyone fails. But fail fast! Learning what does not work is how you achieve success. Embrace struggles, as they will make you stronger and better prepared for future challenges that you cannot see coming. Trust the struggle you are facing now is developing something within you for down the road. You are being prepared.

Be unapologetically yourself. Not everyone will like you, and that's OK. Stay true to who you are and what you believe. People who share your beliefs and passions will find you. Let toxic people go. The five individuals you associate with the most will shape you. Choose your friends wisely. They will have the largest influence on who you become.

Make a difference wherever you can. Get involved in your community and step up when you see opportunities to improve the lives of those around you. My kids joke that I know everyone. For Father's Day one year, they gave me a plaque with the words, "I'm kind of a big deal." I found the more you get involved, the more people's paths you cross, and the greater impact you can have. People will follow someone who has the courage to lead. Jump in and lead where you can. Choosing to step up could start the change that everyone has been waiting to happen. Imagine being the person who organizes the neighborhood cleanup or spearheads the charity drive. Being a big deal isn't about the spotlight; it's about creating ripples of positive change.

What is important to you will evolve. When you are young, you chase material possessions and worry about what others think of you. But as you grow older, you will realize that you have way too much crap, much of which you have no clue how you got it. Eventually, you will only care what the important people in your life think of you. Spending time with your children and grandchildren will become the most precious way to spend your days, as you realize time is a limited resource. The sooner you come to terms with this, the more joy you will have in life.

You only have one chance at living your best life. Fill it with memories of the ones you love and the things that truly matter. When a big wave comes crashing toward you, dive into it. Life is best lived on your own terms, not by waiting for the blows to come to you. Hold yourself accountable for making good decisions but forgive yourself when you make mistakes. Yesterday is gone and can never be redone. Tomorrow is a promise yet to be revealed. Embrace today! It is the only place you can truly live. And always remember, your Dad loves you no matter what!

Mike Elam | Growing My Boys!

Raised by a pastor and teacher, Mike Elam absorbed strong values and a commitment to making a positive impact. After majoring in Radio/TV at Arkansas State University, Mike gained valuable experiences in the Naval Reserve as a Hospital Corpsman. He later returned to Lindenwood University at age 50, underscoring his commitment to lifelong learning.

Entering the broadcast industry in 1982, Mike's career expanded to St. Louis in 1989, encompassing cable TV and the broadband industry. Married to Jennifer since 1991, with three adult children and the "Best Grandson Ever," Mike is an active Rotary member, contributing significantly at local, district, and state levels.

A member of the St. Charles County Council since 2013, Mike envisions the county as a leader in future jobs. Recognized as "The Voice of St. Charles," his influence spans politics, voice-over artistry, and community engagement. Mike's story unfolds as that of a passionate advocate for St. Charles County's prosperous future, embodying a dedication to both personal and community growth.

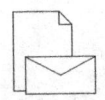

Matt Crossman

Adventure-Filled Fatherhood

The wind whipped against my bare arms and legs, stinging like a thousand paper cuts. Standing next to me, my daughter shivered, and we were equally to blame for our predica … – nah, screw that, it was her dang fault. This polar plunge was her idea, and all I did was encourage her … and be dumb enough to promise to do it with her if nobody else would.

Which, of course, nobody else would because they're too smart to be outside in shorts and T-shirts when it's 25 degrees out.

As we stood on a beach in suburban St. Louis, waiting for our turn to jump in the frigid lake, the emcee prattled on and on. I didn't understand then and still don't now why this event needed an emcee, why he needed to introduce us, and why he needed to prattle on and on when it was 25 degrees out and we were wearing shorts and T-shirts.

We needed to get this over with!

Without introductions!

Or needless prattling!

Finally, he yelled, "Go." I sprinted into the water, spin-jumped, and flopped on my back. Next to me, my daughter sprinted, too, and she dove in headfirst.

The average pool is about 80 degrees.

The water temperature was 39.

The shock felt as if someone waxed my entire back at once. My chest seized as if my skin was suddenly three sizes too small for my rib cage. To my left, my daughter glowed red, and her eyes popped as if they were suddenly three sizes too big for their sockets. We ran together to a building to warm up, and every step on the beach and sidewalk plunged nails deep into our feet.

I was miserably, painfully, desperately cold and proudly bursting because so was my daughter.

As I warmed up in a nearby locker room, I marveled at the profound change in her life, and mine, and what this adventure represented.

When she was about 3, my daughter ascended to the top of a big slide, looked down, and said, "I don't think this is a good idea," and climbed back down. This happened time and again. No matter how I tried to cajole her, reason with her, bribe her, I could not persuade her to go down the slide.

I've been a writer for 30 years, and rule No. 1 in storytelling is, "Show me, don't tell me." That should be rule No.1 in parenting, too. She would learn nothing if I told her what she would get out of going down the slide, if I lectured her about the importance of facing her fears if I explained to her she would build mental strength by doing hard things. But if I showed her those things, she would grow to embody resilience.

The problem was, at the time, I could not show her those things because I did not know those things. I had not lived a life that taught me them. My life had been too easy. I had pursued, and caught, comfort. I had not challenged myself or been challenged.

Soon enough, I learned lessons about perseverance the hard way — when I got laid off from my job at *The Sporting News* magazine.

Even though I knew the layoff was coming, I was wholly unprepared for it. Faced with life in turbulent water, I nearly drowned because I didn't know how to swim in anything but a pool.

Fear consumed me as I pursued a career as a freelance writer, and that fear made me timid. I lived as if I was atop the slide and unwilling to go down it ... but also unable to walk back down the ladder because there was no ladder. I had no choice but to take the ride in front of me.

That fear is still there, sometimes, like a yell echoing across a canyon. But I learned to face fears in the professional world by facing fears in the physical world. I constructed a mantra: *If I can persevere through hardship when I choose that hardship and can quit at any time, I will be that much more prepared to endure hardship when it chooses me and I can't quit.*

I went rock climbing and ice climbing and surfing and white-water rafting and ziplining and to dog-mushing school and climbed a 60-foot red oak named Willa. I competed in Tough Mudder and adventure races and organized my own endurance events — three 250-mile bike rides across Missouri and an event I dubbed 50-50-50, in which nine friends and I hiked 50 miles, biked 50 miles, and canoed 50 miles, all in one epic weekend to celebrate my 50th birthday.

The morning after, I came downstairs and my daughter said, "Dad, you look terrible!"

I considered that a high compliment ... and proof that I was showing her important lessons I could never adequately tell her.

The world teaches us to crave comfort, to bask in ease, to always seek the path of least resistance. But we grow most when we push ourselves, when we strive for goals that are just out of our reach, when we doubt whether can do something and try anyway.

Over the past 10 years, I have tried to live a life that shows my two daughters that.

The only problem is ... well, I kind of wish I hadn't.

Because watching them live like that is going to put me in an early grave.

First it was skiing. I was shocked they wanted to go, shocked again when they strapped on the skis for lessons and gobsmacked when I couldn't get them to leave even as night fell.

Then I nearly froze to death in Lake St. Louis, and after that came a trip to Colorado so I could write a family vacation story. I called it "He Thrills, They Chill." I planned to go rock climbing and hiking while my wife and daughters made jam and petted animals and did experiments looking for evidence of pollution in creeks. I hoped to coax them onto the thrill side, but I wasn't expecting much.

A sure sign that a day is going to be good is if I have to sign a waiver, wear a helmet, or use a carabiner. When I have to do all three, I know it's going to be epic. What I didn't realize was how difficult it would be to have my daughters alongside me for such an adventure.

It's one thing to encourage your kids to live a life of adventure, to face their fears, to build perseverance by doing hard things. It's quite another to snap their carabiners in place, make sure their helmets fit, and then watch them navigate danger.

I mean, they could get hurt!

And so could I!

And their mom would kill me!

But chickening out would have been disastrous, so I scribbled my name on the waiver next to the printed version of mine …

AND THEIRS!

WHICH WAS SO MUCH HARDER!

… and double- and triple-checked their equipment. Every helmet was too small or too big or not padded enough or whatever — it was clear whoever makes these things doesn't know the first thing about protecting my girls' precious brains. Anyway, when I made the final snap of her harness — I ALMOST FORGOT TO TELL YOU ABOUT THE

HARNESS — to make sure it was properly tightened, my hand slipped, and I bonked her face ...

SO HARD!

... I thought I broke both her nose.

Nervous, who, me?

We turned our attention to the ropes course at Winter Park Adventure Quest. The apparatus looked like a jungle gym as imagined by the set designer for *Lord of the Rings*. Wires and rope bridges and planks ringed the two-story structure.

Imagine being two stories off the ground and facing a series of ropes shaped like giant U's hanging from a crossbar overhead. To get across, you step from one rope to the next.

My daughter stood on one end of the obstacle. I stood on the other. She asked me how to do it. I offered my best guess but did not try to show her because I couldn't deal with my own fears, my girls' fears, and my fears on their behalf at the same time.

For a minute, two, three, she couldn't move. She wanted to give up. She wanted to go. She wanted to give up. She wanted to go. I thought she was going to climb back down, just like she did on the slide. But she didn't. After instruction from the guide, she not only tried, she finished.

Sunshine shot out of her ears!

Lightning bolts shot from her fingertips!

Relief shot out of every one of my pores!

Then she climbed down off the ropes course and scaled the adjacent rock wall before I could even get down to watch her.

Who's teaching whom about the joys of risk-taking, I have wondered over and over again since then. Now when she's not jumping in frigid lakes or scaling rock walls, she's acting in local theater productions, which requires an entirely different kind of fear-facing and yet also jacks up my heart rate at the same time.

Do I want my daughters to live adventurous lives? Unequivocally yes!

Do I want to witness any of it? Unequivocally no!

It scares me half-stupid, and I know from experience that the only way I can get over that fear is to force myself to watch them do it over and over again … (and keels over of a heart attack).

Actually, they don't have to show me. They can just tell me later.

Matt Crossman has been a journalist for 30 years. He met his wife, Emily, at a newspaper in Pennsylvania. He covered city hall, and she covered the courthouse. She turned her experience into a career as a lawyer. He turned his experience into … more experience as a journalist. They have two daughters and live in suburban St. Louis.

In pursuit of stories, Matt has jumped out of an airplane, hiked with soldiers training to be Green Berets, and spent a summer playing the same par-3 golf course over and over again in pursuit of his first hole in one. He still can't believe shot 1,589 went in.

Matt's work has been cited by Best American Sports Writing, Best American Essays, and Year's Best Sports Writing. His claim to fame is he is the only staff writer in the 127-year history of *The Sporting News* to appear on the cover. He had to jam a plastic car in his mouth to do so, but that hasn't stopped him from bragging about it.

Prentice Robertson

Lessons in Servant Leadership

The greatest servant leader ever to walk the earth was Jesus, who served all of mankind throughout His life to the point of sacrificing Himself unto death upon a cross. There will never be a greater example of a servant leader for us to follow. If you were to set out to write a book on the 100 greatest leaders of all time, you would land on at least 95 who achieved their leadership prowess by humbly serving others, with the rare exceptions of a narcissistic dictator, military commander, or business tycoon.

The definition of servant leadership is simple — serve those whom you lead. Never ask them to do something you wouldn't be willing to do yourself. Follow the golden rule from the Good Book of treating people the way you would want to be treated. God has blessed me by entrusting me with two important groups of people to lead — my family of five and my work family of 45,000. I love and cherish both. My family is made up of a wonderful wife of nearly four decades, a married daughter who has provided me with two precious grandchildren, and twin sons who are not yet married as of this writing. My work family consists of employees across all 48 contiguous states for whom I feel a similar responsibility of fatherhood as I do with my own kids.

In my company, we refer to this philosophy of servant leadership as the inverted organizational structure — where the bigger titles are at the bottom of the org chart, supporting up to the front-line employees at the top who directly serve our clients as ambassadors. In my family, as is the case with most dads, this inverted philosophy could be depicted as a desire to see our kids ascend to greater heights than we ever did by praying for them to live life with the fullness and abundance that God promises to those who love Him and are called according to His good purposes.

Unfortunately, in today's society, this mindset feels a bit counterintuitive to the selfish worldview of "looking out for No. 1." But if there is one thing I have discovered through the years, it is that I learn more from those I lead than they learn from me. A real-life case in point occurred at a recent awards ceremony in my company, where employees nominated each other for leadership awards. As I spent time reading the amazing comments people wrote about each other, it became easy to formulate a job description for a servant leader that came directly from the descriptions in these nominations. Here is my attempt at a compilation of the best comments using their actual words in a handful of sentences:

"He/she is a selfless leader, who has a desire to help his/her team be successful and develop them to be the best versions of themselves while treating everyone as the most important person on the team. He/she leads by example by always being first in the office and last to leave, holding to a high standard while showing respect, support, and encouragement to others. He/she always has the team's back, going to bat for them and shooting straight with them in complete transparency. He/she works tirelessly to keep the team up to our standard beyond the standard and motivates with positive reinforcement to create a winning culture. He/she listens to the team and is a true mentor. His/her commitment to our core values emboldens each employee to earn our place by simply doing what is right. He/she is a true ambassador of the organization."

Wow! Forget about the classroom definition of a servant leader — no dictionary could have said it better than our employees did about their leaders. What an amazing testament to the strength of the leaders in my company.

In my family, this notion of a leader listening to or learning from a subordinate often takes the form of the child becoming the parent and the parent becoming the child. Even though my job as dad was to teach my kids as their leader, I could recount dozens of times this phenomenon occurred with my three children when they were younger. I will attempt to distill this reversal of roles down to one example from each of them that resounds in a special way for me as their dad.

My daughter has always had a strong personality, which she has channeled in adulthood into being a great mom, wife, and creative director of a major branding agency. She is also strong in her faith. This strength really shined more than ever when she was in middle school, and our family had a big life decision to make. I had left a job and was considering multiple offers for my next job — two of which were secure positions where we could avoid moving, and the third of which was risky and would require us to move away from the only place we had ever called home to another part of the country.

The simple path would have been to take one of the secure jobs that would keep us in our comfort zone of home, but I really sensed God leading me to the riskier path that would require a move. In fact, the night before I had to give the three prospective employers my decision, I took the kids for Chinese food. When I cracked open my fortune cookie, the fortune message was, "When choosing from multiple paths, choose the westerly route." You guessed it — the state where we would be moving is to the west. If you don't think God can speak to you in many ways, He can apparently do so even through a fortune cookie!

But even after that divine confirmation, I was still feeling cold feet about asking the family to pick up and move away from the only place we had ever known. Later that night, we had a family meeting, and I told them that I was leaning toward taking one of the safer options and keeping us home. Enter Scene 1 of the parent becoming the child and the child becoming the parent. My daughter — with the most to lose as a middle-school girl, popular, established with her friends, and captain of the cheerleader squad — proceeded to scold me for wimping out. She looked at my wife and me and reminded us that the move would be an adventure for our family that God had already ordained. How could we go wrong with God on our side? And so, my eighth-grade daughter lovingly slapped me back to reality and gave me the courage to take the leap of faith and move the family. A move that God has blessed and prospered beyond my wildest imagination. What a learning experience for a dad from his daughter.

Scene 2 shifts to a golf course where one of my twin sons was competing for the state golf championship. It was his senior year in high school with no plans of playing collegiately or professionally, so this was truly his last hurrah in competitive golf. As an avid sports fan and sports dad, I admittedly lived a bit too vicariously through the athletic exploits of my boys. The tournament was a two-day, 36-hole event, and after the first round my son was in the top four of 100 participants placing him in the last group teeing off the next day. His second round was also going very well, and as we approached the 16th tee box, I suspected he was leading the tournament after 33 holes. Suddenly, the proverbial golf gods struck. His tee shot barely clipped a tree limb and ricocheted deep into the woods. A couple of bad decisions later, and he had a double bogey on a par 5, losing at least two strokes to the rest of the field. He then showed his mettle by rebounding on the next hole, nearly holing out on a par three over water.

Then on 18, he hit his tee shot too good as it rolled into a fairway bunker that should have been out of his reach. As we approached the bunker, it was evident his ball had embedded under the lip of the bunker, and his only shot was to blast out sideways, which took any chance of parring the hole away. Those tough breaks on the last few holes not only cost him the state championship he had worked so hard for, but knocked him just out of the top 10 medal spots at state.

As my son and I stood side by side and watched the closing ceremony with ten kids getting medals whom he had been leading three holes before, my heart was absolutely breaking for him. I didn't see a teenager in that moment. I saw my little boy who had been dealt an unfair hand to the point that I was fighting back tears and just wanted to protect him. Until the child once again became the parent, as he looked at me after the medal ceremony and said, "You know, Dad, being the 11th best golfer in the state of Missouri isn't bad, is it?" Wow! I realized I wasn't comforting him; rather, he was comforting me with a mature perspective that was wise beyond his years. He turned my tears of sadness for him into incredible pride in my son as he grew up before my very eyes while teaching me about humility and gratitude that was truly inspiring.

Scene 3 moves to my other twin son and is the most poignant of all. It goes all the way back to the birth of the boys when one of them was born with significant health concerns. He battled through numerous surgeries early in his life, and my wife and I were told he would probably never have much strength in his lower extremities. Watching your little baby, toddler, and little boy go through what he went through was gut-wrenching for my wife and me. As the budding sports dad, it was difficult to know that one twin would have struggles that the other would not have to contend with. But God blessed my son with a can-do attitude and a winning mentality. As he grew older, he not only gained strength, but became a very good athlete in his own right, which taught me that championships in life can be won in many ways. It was inspiring watching him scrap for loose balls, drill three-pointers on the basketball court, and develop one of the most beautiful golf swings I have ever seen. Once again, one of my kids taught me far more than I could have ever taught him as he chose not to live under his circumstances but instead rose above them.

So what is the moral to this particular chapter of this book of wisdom? Here it is — regardless of whether it's your kids, employees, players, or students, lead them by serving them. In the process, you will not only be a blessing to them in supporting their development, but they will teach you more than you could ever learn on your own.

Prentice Robertson | Lessons in Servant Leadership

Prentice Robertson was born and raised in Georgia, a proud graduate and unabashed fan of the University of Georgia. He has spent his entire career in progressive leadership roles in the staffing and security industry, culminating in his current role as U.S. President and COO of the largest privately-owned security services company in the world — GardaWorld.

With 45,000-plus employees under his care and responsibility, Prentice has always been a growth entrepreneur who prides himself in building organizations with highly employee-centric cultures and best-in-class customer service. He has also served in leadership positions in faith-based organizations such as Upward Sports, AWANA, and C-12, an organization of Christian business leaders. But his greatest source of joy comes from his wife, three kids, two grandchildren and personal relationship with Jesus Christ.

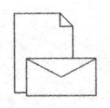

Brad Dempsey

The Power In You

This chapter is dedicated to my dad, Tom Dempsey. A simple man from a small town in northeast Missouri. He married his high school sweetheart, Alice Mae Dimmitt, and has two sons, me and my younger brother, Brent. A carpenter by trade and my youth sports coach, my dad never missed one of our games and has always showed up when we've needed him. He's been a dad of great character and is now Grandad to my kids Alice, Aubrie, and Quinn, my nephew Mack, and my niece Nellie Mae.

I hope this chapter encourages you to use the power of the lessons you have learned through your life's story. I believe each of our stories is made to be uniquely ours and to bring us together. As I share a snapshot of my story, please remember that comparison is the thief of joy. I share only to give you a perspective and provide you with value as you move forward on your journey.

It was September 9, 2008, and my wife, Gala, and I had wrapped up our workday and were going through our nightly routine in preparation for the next day. It was a few months earlier when we had gotten married. As we went to bed that night, we did so in my parents' home. Yes, that same room in the basement that my dad finished for me so I could have my own space throughout my teenage years.

In March of that year, my mother, Alice, was diagnosed with Stage-4 colon cancer. Gala and I had moved in to help support my mom and dad. Mom had deferred on going through chemo and other medical options and instead chose to stay on Winding River Ranch in Grand Lake, Col with a woman named Elaine Busse. The same woman who had saved my life a few years earlier. Mom's decision wasn't popular amongst family and friends, but I understood it. I believe that deep down inside our souls, it was something we understood together. A bond that spiritually connects us to this very day.

I woke up on September 10 to take my shower. Except this time, it was different. Every morning, my dad and I would exchange good mornings as he headed upstairs, and then I took my turn in the shower. Something was completely off that morning, and I could feel it. I jolted up the stairs to find my dad, and I heard a loud moaning followed by crying. I walked into my dad's room and found him on his knees. He looked at me and said she was gone. Not only was she gone, when I looked at my dad, he looked as if a part of his soul had been ripped out of him. I had never in my life remembered seeing my dad show emotion remotely close to this. It was a permanent change in our lives that we never could have prepared ourselves for.

Following mom's passing, Gala and I decided life was too short, and we weren't going to waste any time in starting a family. A short 10 months later, on July 7, 2009, Gala gave birth to a baby girl, Alice. Yes, after her grandmother. What a whirlwind! There had been so much adversity, uncertainty, and pain that came before that moment in my life, but on that day, it was all worth it. I had become a dad.

It was June 5, 1996, and my best buddy, Shelby, and I went fishing with his brother and a few others at a local spot. Little did I know my life and the lives of my parents would change forever that day. On the way home, the driver ran a four-way stop, and we were struck directly in the side by an oncoming vehicle. I was sitting behind the back seat of a small Ford Bronco where there was no seatbelt and was ejected out of the back. They found me a good distance from the vehicle unconscious and in a life-threatening condition. I was life-flighted to the University of Missouri-Columbia Hospital, and the medical team saved my life. Following my hospitalization, I returned home to heal from my physical injuries, but we weren't aware that the traumatic brain injury I suffered would bring a lifetime of challenges.

In the 1990s, brain research wasn't as advanced, so my parents had quite an uphill battle. I spent my teenage years in and out of doctors' offices with a handful of stops to psychiatric units of hospitals, being heavily medicated and in a world of internal pain. I went through a consistent cycle of anger, depression, fatigue, and sadness. What was amazing about my life was I was blessed. I had friends, I was an athlete, and I had a girlfriend. I met my wife, Gala, the school year after my accident. Our lockers were next to each other. My last name is Dempsey; her last name is Dempsey. No relation, just a 13-year-old brain-injured young man dating a young woman who was adopted out of foster care at age 4. Our relationship was quite the roller-coaster ride as teenagers and into our early 20s. We've both learned over the years that trauma doesn't go away. It takes constant, consistent intentional work to persevere and overcome.

Throughout my teenage years, my parents endured an onslaught of never knowing what was coming next, but they never stopped loving me. Mom was my savior, but my relationship with Dad was strained. I was always stuck in the mindset that he didn't get me and didn't want to understand me. In fact, a majority of the time, I was awful to both of them. One time, I was so angry that I tossed my dad across the kitchen. I'll never forget the look in his eyes after that happened. I was ashamed and felt extreme guilt but, unfortunately, that was my reality. The reality of me telling my mother every day I just want to feel good. The piling up of medical bills, the holes in walls in the basement, my consistent anger at the world, and my impulsive behavior. For most people this part of me was not seen, but my parents lived it, and I can only imagine what it was like to be them.

At 22, I went cold turkey on my medications and went through what doctors equated to heroin withdrawal. I ended up at the Mayo Clinic in Jacksonville, Fla., and to this day feel like I'm still recovering from what those medications did to me. However, it really was the start of my life coming together. Soon after, my mom found Eliane Busse, that beautiful woman in the mountains of Colorado who just turned 100 years old as I write this. She saved my life through nutrition and the word of God. I guess that gives you a small glimpse of why my mom wanted to go there to pass on to heaven. Amazingly enough, after my guardian angel mother passed, my life started to make sense. I became a dad. I became a teacher and coach, and I was on the path to finding purpose in my life.

Gala and I had two more children, our daughter Aubrie, and our son Quinn. I've been blessed to teach and or coach kindergarteners through seniors in college, and I now have my own business. Along the way, I've had the opportunity to build so many lifelong relationships. All while managing, surviving, and thriving through chronic depression, fatigue, and pain. It has been mentally and physically exhausting. So many days, I want to quit. Since my teenage years, I've always had thoughts about taking my life, but for me, I've learned not to let God's training ground become Satan's playground. The significant importance of that is the responsibility I have as a child of God. The desire and drive I have to love and provide value to my children. Through it all, being a dad has been the most challenging aspect of my life. Learning to be the dad my kids need has been beyond anything I could ever do alone. If only there were an instruction book on exactly how to be a father. But wait ... there is ... and it is full of Good News.

As a dad, you truly are a part of something bigger than yourself, and to be a part of something bigger than yourself, you have to lead yourself well. I've learned the importance of teaching children that being a great person of high moral character will never go out of style. Being a good teammate — whether at home, on a sports team, a member of the choir, or in the workplace — will always be of utmost importance.

Anything I've been able to accomplish as a dad is because my father and the community of great fathers, I've surrounded myself with have led me to want to know my father in heaven. It truly is mission critical to find a great mentor(s) and surround yourself with a positive, thriving community.

My encouragement is to always show up with love in your heart. God is love and your children spell love T-I-M-E. Love demands effort and requires forgiveness. With small steps at a steady pace, you have the opportunity to improve every day. Know that your spiritual, mental, and physical health, and wellness are what make you complete. Not perfect, but complete. The type of completeness that allows you to align your spirit with the Holy Spirit so you can maximize your potential through the plan God has for you. Let go of your EGO (Edging God Out) and know adversity doesn't make you weak or strong; it reveals who you really are deep down inside when nobody's looking. There are blessings on the other side of adversity. Be prayerful, be purposeful, and be intentional. Your blessings are on the way.

Isaiah 40:31, "Those who wait on the Lord, shall renew their strength; they shall mount up with wings like eagles, they shall run and not be weary, they shall walk and not faint.

Brad Dempsey | The Power In You

Brad Dempsey is a personal and leadership development coach, a motivational speaker, an author, and an entrepreneur. He's spent his life learning to survive and thrive through challenges brought on by a traumatic brain injury he suffered in an accident at age 13. Brad is a teacher and facilitator of what he calls the "Power of 3 Relationships." The spiritual relationship, the relationship with self and relationships with others.

Brad was born and raised in Hannibal, Mo. He holds a bachelor's of science degree in psychology and a master's of education degree in athletic administration. He spent 12 years in education as a teacher, coach, and administrator. In 2018, Brad received the Outstanding Young Alumnus Award from Hannibal LaGrange University for his work with young people and for his service to his community.

In 2018, Brad started Stourney LLC, a company built on the foundation of sharing stories to improve journeys. In 2021, Brad launched Mindset Sports, a coaching company for athletes. In 2024, he founded The Leadership Commitment and rebranded Mindset Sports to the Leadership Sports Academy. Brad also contracts with other leadership companies throughout the United States.

Brad married Gala in 2008. They have three children, Alice, Aubrie, and Quinn. His greatest joys are practicing his faith, loving his family, forming relationships that last a lifetime, and building strong sustainable communities.

Jeff Erdmann

Different Perspectives

Mom was a go-go dancer. Carol had fiery-red bouffant hair, high heels, and a two-piece bikini dripping in sequins. I have the video to prove it. At just under 5 feet tall, she caught the eye of a certain rock-and-roll bass player named Terry, who looked like Buddy Holly but with movie star good looks and a charismatic smile. You can guess the rest.

This all happened in Fargo, N.D. They got married, had me, and my dad joined a successful band with regular gigs in Los Angeles and Las Vegas. He was a working, professional musician. We moved west.

A few years later, my parents realized that they were different people with different perspectives on life. Six-year-old me didn't understand why my dad only came by occasionally to our new apartment and why he seemed so sad.

Then, my mom met Mike, a Navy veteran who worked for a custom cabinet shop. Mike was a strong, soft-spoken man who enjoyed beer, cigarettes, and building things made of wood. He had a tattoo of a mouse "shooting" dice with a cue stick on his forearm. He and my dad were so different in so many ways.

Mike and his business partner opened The Cabinet Guild in Chatsworth, Calif., which became a successful business, catering to high-end, occasionally famous clients as well as some Vegas casinos. He was hardworking and reliable.

But we rarely talked.

When we did talk, it was usually about something mundane or utilitarian. We generally didn't share many interests or viewpoints. I was a musician! I didn't have time for power tools. But he let me use his truck frequently for transporting my bass equipment to the next backyard gig. I can't remember if I ever thanked him.

I would visit my dad on the weekends like most kids with divorced parents. He had a zero-bedroom studio apartment in east Hollywood, across the street from Los Angeles City College. Not a great neighborhood, but as a kid, it was like a giant playground. I would ride my skateboard all over the campus whether Terry was there or not. It didn't seem dangerous back then.

Dad moved into a bigger apartment nearby when he got his English degree from UCLA.

When I was about 13, Terry started working in the mail room at Columbia Pictures. He became the private secretary for the president of 20th Century Fox, whose office was next to the publicity department. My dad was (and is) outgoing, eloquent, and never afraid to strike up a conversation with anyone no matter how famous they are. He would chat with the publicists and even answer phones for them when they went to lunch.

On the weekends, he would give me private tours of the backlots of Fox, Warner Bros., MGM, and Paramount. It always felt like he owned the place. We were walking through Burbank Studios one day, and Terry told me a story about my mom's brother, Rick. When Rick was a teenager in Fargo, he shot a short 8mm film that won a young filmmaker's award. (And, yes, he shot the footage of my mom go-go dancing!) Rick's parents, my grandparents, were very strict Baptists, and they did not support his "hobby." My dad tried to convince Rick to go out into the world with a camera and show everyone what he could do. But that never happened. Rick became an aluminum siding salesman. My dad looked at me on the front steps of the Columbia Pictures building and said, "Your uncle Rick should be here right now, doing this. Don't hide your light under a bush."

I was 18. My picture was on the cover of the local newspaper wearing a cap and gown, beaming happily as a newly minted high school graduate. Not long afterward, my mom approached me. She said Mike wanted me to move out. I can't blame Mike for wanting me to find my own place. I would realize much later that it was probably the best thing he could have done for me at the time.

I rented a room from my drummer's mom for a while. But everything seemed stagnant in the suburbs. I called my dad asking if he would mind if I crashed on his couch in Los Angeles. He went beyond that and offered to have me move in as roommates.

Terry was now a unit publicist at 20th Century Fox. His job required traveling to dozens of cities to show previews of upcoming movies to huge crowds at sci-fi conventions. Speaking in front of a thousand people seemed to come naturally to him. At one convention, he met a magazine editor named Paula. They would start meeting in places like New York or Chicago for dinner dates. Paula eventually moved to California, got a position at Paramount, and they bought a condo together a mountain range away, over Cahuenga Pass in the San Fernando Valley. I now had the L.A. apartment all to myself.

To pay the bills, I worked at the Museum of Contemporary Art in downtown Los Angeles while simultaneously taking classes at Los Angeles City College. Music. English. Electronics. Music again. I played bass with several jazz groups around town and at the college. I considered becoming a professional musician in L.A., but there was just too much competition. Those studio cats could play circles around me.

One of my college friends wanted to tour a campus in the central California beach town of Santa Cruz, and because I was the one with a car, I drove us the six hours up the 101. We all took a tour of this beautiful, idyllic collection of colleges nestled in the redwoods above Monterey Bay. I spontaneously decided to move to Santa Cruz, got a job manufacturing electronic gizmos, and took more classes at nearby Cabrillo Community College.

At this point in my life, I had not proved that I could see anything through to the end. So, having spent five years at two community colleges studying four different majors, I decided at the age of 25 to actually finish college. I transferred from Cabrillo to UC Santa Cruz as a "re-entry" student due to my advanced years, majoring in English literature. Two years later, I invited my mom and Mike up to attend my graduation. As I was receiving my diploma along with my Phi Beta Kappa key, Mike turned to my mom and said, "I wish we had done more for Jeff."

But Mike showed me what it meant to put in the hard work necessary to build a career, family, and home. He showed me it was possible to make a decision and stick by it. He quit smoking and drinking years earlier, cold turkey. I never expected to learn life lessons from this "other" dad. He gave me so much.

Over Christmas break, before graduating, I flew down to SoCal. My dad invited me to the set of the movie he was working on, "Encino Man." He introduced me to the sound mixer, Bob, and we hit it off. We were both tech enthusiasts with an English degree and had the same goofy sense of humor. Bob asked me to be part of his crew when I completed my degree, and I accepted immediately. This would lead to an 18-year career as a boom operator. I also met my wife, Joyce, on that same first gig. Had it not been for Terry, I never would have had the opportunity to establish that rapport with Bob, nor would I have met the love of my life.

After I left the film business, Joyce and I bought houses to rehab. I had somehow collected enough power tools to do most of the work myself, and the internet was a great source of DIY information. Now that they were retired, Mom told me Mike would be interested in helping with our current project, so we flew them out to join us in St. Louis for a few weeks. Mike and I now had common ground, something we both enjoyed. He was a master craftsman with 40 years of experience. I learned a lot from him in those two weeks. Even though we were still very different people, I felt closer to Mike than I ever had before.

Jeff Erdmann | Different Perspectives

Jeff Erdmann graduated from the University of California, Santa Cruz, in 1992 with a bachelor's degree in English literature and a Phi Beta Kappa key. Within a few months, he found himself working in Los Angeles as a television and motion picture sound technician. This is when he would also meet a costumer named Joyce. Thirty-two years later they are still on their first date.

After 18 years in the movie business, Jeff transitioned to real estate investing and home remodeling, where he and Joyce did most of the work themselves, bringing abused and neglected homes back to life. Joyce is especially proud of her plaster work.

Jeff also had a brief career as a wine salesman and now works with the nation's leading VA mortgage lender. His nickname at the office is "the chameleon."

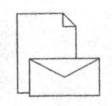

Matt White

The Gift of Being a Dad

Dear Brandon and Anna,

Thank you for the gift of getting to be your dad. Parenting has been and continues to be an amazing journey. You two and your mom know my shortcomings as a dad better than anyone. Yet, you continue to love me unconditionally and show me support. Your mom is the most amazing supporter of all. If every husband had a wife like her and every kid had a mom like her, the world would be a better place.

I hope you have the opportunity to have your own parenting journey someday. If so, you'll see that the trip has both the downhill coast and the uphill climb. However, it is worth every mile! Along the way, your mom and I have learned important lessons. I want to share a few with you and with any other parents who could use them.

Judgment

Parents feel judged based on the actions of their kids. Just ask one, and I bet they will agree. I know I often judge parents, for good or bad. When I see a teenager holding the door for a stranger or helping a neighbor pick up leaves in the yard, I think, "Those parents raised him right." When I see a toddler in a shopping cart throwing a tantrum in front of the whole store, I think, "Wow! That's a parent who has lost control of his or her kid!" Any parent would admit that parenting is not easy. When you see the actions of a kid in the future, I would suggest you offer praise to a parent whose kid has done something well. They probably need encouragement. When the kid is being a brat, try to be understanding and pray for both the kid and the parent. We can all use it!

Accept Advice

Our independence can cause us to want to forge our own trail and ignore the experiences of those who have gone before us. No parents are perfect, although you know your grandparents on both sides are pretty close. They were wise beyond their years and always seemed to have the right answers. My mom and dad modeled the right way to raise a family. We weren't wealthy, but love abounded. Then, I met Mom and saw the same qualities in her family. I wish every kid had the kind of example that our parents have given us. I learned some of the most important leadership skills from Mark, my previous boss and mentor. At church, I have tried to emulate the example of many friends who are a stage or two ahead of me. Remember, it is much easier to learn from someone else's mistakes than to go through them ourselves.

Pray Hard

I was talking to a pastor friend after church one day. He has three kids and is a more experienced parent than me. I asked him about parenting, and I expected some step-by-step instructions on how to do it the right way. Instead, what he shared really stuck with me. He said he spent A LOT of time praying for his kids. It caused me to realize that while we say and do things that have an influence on you, God has unlimited resources to shape you, convict you when you're doing wrong, and prompt you to make the right decisions. Since that conversation, I have made praying for you a higher priority. I thank the Lord when you are doing well. I pray hard for you when you need extra help. I also have peace that comes from knowing God loves you, cares about you, has perfect timing, and is a much more capable Father than I am.

Brandon, with your analytical mind and desire to pursue a field in computer science or engineering, I prayed that as you left for college, you would see the evidence for your faith and not be convinced by many in your field that there is only a physical realm and not a spiritual one. God answered this prayer. You attended a strong Christian university, are organizing Bible studies with your wife, and are serving at school and your church. Your faith is stronger than ever!

Anna, with your fun-loving nature, enjoyment of entertainment, and spending time with friends, I prayed you would carve out time to read your Bible, spend time in prayer, and make your faith a priority. God answered this prayer, also. You bought a study Bible and got involved in Fellowship of Christian Athletes, attended a Bible study with friends, and started serving in the Children's Ministry at church. I realized how important your faith was to you. You cannot imagine how proud you both make me!

Show and Tell

Kids need to be told what to do. Without being told, they are often left without direction. There were times I got upset with you for breaking a rule that you never even knew was a rule, because I neglected to discuss it with you. Make it clear what your expectations are. This can yield immediate results. Additionally, if you want a lasting impact, show kids what to do. It may take years of consistently doing the right thing in front of kids for it to stick, but it is worth the investment.

Extend Grace

This is an area where I struggled, especially when you were younger. I expected you to always listen, never disobey, or never have a bad day. Instead of recognizing that you would have missteps every now and then, I continued to push for perfection. From time to time, your grandparents would remind me that I was being too hard on you, and I would pridefully push ahead with a mindset of, "These are my kids, and I'll take care of it as I see fit." Instead, I should have learned earlier to extend grace.

We never had big problems with you like drug or alcohol abuse, trouble with the law, or something else major. I hope you never have those issues with your kids. But, if you do, or if you know someone else who does, remember to extend grace. Sometimes, there is nothing we can do to convince someone to change. However, there is someone who can, and we should take our concerns to Him in prayer.

Uniqueness

Sometimes, I think parenting would be a whole lot easier if our kids had the same interests, same personality, and same temperament that we do. However, we are all unique. While there may be similarities, there are often a lot of differences among parents and their kids. Brandon, you loved fixing things — cars, boats, computers, and cell phones — nearly your whole life. This is something Mom and I knew very little about. Anna, you developed a love for playing lacrosse, a sport we knew nothing about and still don't understand all that well! It may be tempting to try to get our kids to fit into our mold, but they will probably be miserable being forced to do the things that we like best. I know I would have been if my parents would have done that to me.

Never Give Up

Sometimes, we want kids to be robots, always following the correct pre-programmed steps. Or, we wish we could make the right moves for them. Observe a youth sporting event. Mom or Dad is in the stands hollering, "No, Johnny, not that way, fake right, then go left!" The only thing better than watching Johnny play ball would be to have a remote control for Johnny so we could control his every move. However, kids have their own minds. Sometimes, kids behave poorly because they forget the right thing to do or have a momentary lapse in judgment. Other times, they willfully disobey. There may be times when you feel that a certain behavior will never change. Whatever you do, don't give up. Why? Because I have seen multiple times that kids and adults come around, sometimes long after I had given up hope.

One final story from our experience raising kids. Mom and I both enjoyed the academic side of school, even though Mom got better grades than me. I think you would probably both admit that academics were not a passion for you in grade school. We tried convincing you that there was a payoff to working hard for good grades. It would help you get better college scholarships.

Brandon, you started turning it on during your last three semesters of high school. You also studied hard for the ACT. In the end, you earned a full-tuition scholarship to the college you most wanted to attend. Anna, you also started taking your academics more seriously toward the end of high school. You went a different route. You worked on your athletic skills and focused on lacrosse. You played during the regular high school season and also played on off-season teams, getting exposure to college coaches in the state. You kept in close contact with the coach of your most desired college. Showing a lot of maturity, you navigated this whole process yourself. In the end, you got a great combined athletic and academic scholarship! I say all this not to brag (well, maybe just a bit of bragging) but to convince you to never give up on someone. The way you started your academic career was in stark contrast to the wonderful way you finished.

I want to conclude this letter the same way I started — by thanking you. It is so cool that we get to be your parents! God could have given you to many other parents if He had wanted to. What a blessing it is that He gave you to Mom and me.

Love,
Dad

Matt White | The Gift of Being a Dad

Matt White is a lifelong Missourian who resides in Lake Saint Louis with his incredible wife, Jill. They have been blessed with a grown son and his wife, who are college students, and a daughter who's headed to college soon. They have a small poodle who should author a book on negotiating tactics, as she always seems to get her way.

Matt works in the field of radiation oncology as a medical physicist. It is a rewarding career that allows him to work with some amazing people and equipment. Outside of work, he loves spending time with family and friends. Matt's favorite pastimes include boating and water sports, eating sushi, running and bike riding, playing board games, and catching up with family he doesn't get to see often enough. Matt and his family enjoy time in their local church, realizing that all good things come from the Lord.

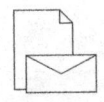

Mark Hollander

It's a Boy ...

As I look back over my life, I don't think there is anything I wanted to be more than a dad. The thought of having a little life to raise and shape was so overwhelmingly powerful to me. I remember lying in bed at night and dreaming about playing catch with my son and coaching little league teams. I always had such a tremendous relationship with my dad that I could only imagine it would be incredible to do the same with my little boy one day.

When my wife was pregnant for the first time, I was overjoyed. I could think of nothing else, and I became the most attentive and doting husband of all time. I knew I was already taking care of my whole family by being a better husband and providing for her every need. I could not wait until the day my little boy would be born.

After nine long months of waiting, the day finally arrived. It was an incredibly hot day in early June 1985. Contractions started late in the evening and continued into the very early morning hours. We made a few phone calls to let the close family know that the time had come, and we loaded the car and headed to the hospital. We arrived and made our way through the emergency room and were admitted. Dilated only a couple of centimeters, the nurses confirmed that my wife was indeed in labor, but it would take some time.

The hospital was hot — it seemed unbearable. Walking the halls to get the contractions to come faster and to help dilate more was our task. Doing so made my wife's water break, yet it seemed like it was taking forever. Contractions came more quickly, and dilation happened faster, and then — finally — it was time.

Push hard now … but as she did, the heart rate dropped substantially. The baby was in distress, and emergency steps had to be taken. Nurses rushed in and told me to put my camera away. I may not want pictures of this scary moment. The umbilical cord was wrapped around his neck, and I took a step backward against the wall and watched as nurses rushed around my wife to help. Before I knew it, the baby was out, and I heard his first cries. Although petrifying, my baby boy was out and seemed OK. I yelled at the top of my lungs, "It's a boy!" The doctor looked down at my nearly-blue little child and said, "I have done this before, and this is a little girl!"

I was so sure that my dream child would be a boy that I was fully convinced that there was no way in the world that I would have a daughter but here SHE was. She was all mine.

Fast-forward now nearly 40 years, and I received the most amazing gift of a daughter who has given me hundreds of softball games to manage and "run hugs" that still make my heart full. I could never have dreamt that my "son" would end up being the most amazing daughter that I could have ever hoped for. She is my Sunshine, my only Sunshine, and I wouldn't trade her for an entire team of sons.

My wife and I had a second little girl nearly nine years later. This one was a blue-eyed beauty with strawberry-blonde hair—the perfect little angel with little rosebud lips. There were no crazy complications at birth, and we did an ultrasound this time to verify the sex of the baby, so there would be no surprises this time!

This little girl seemed to be sick all of the time—lots and lots of crying and sleepless nights. We spent week after week making appointments to see the doctor, and we were pumping amoxicillin prescriptions into her frequently. The doctors kept telling us she just had sinus problems and would grow out of it. Developmentally, she was good, but she seemed to take longer to talk and walk than our first child. "They are all a little different," everyone told us. We tried to be patient, but she was sick. All. The. Time.

Our nurse friend suggested that we make an appointment with an ear, nose, and throat doctor to get a second opinion. At the time, it was a big deal to visit a specialist because it required that we get a special referral, and the copayments were much more. We scheduled the appointment and made the visit. The doctor did one test and then insisted that we take our child immediately to St. Louis Children's Hospital. "Don't go home to get a change of clothes or anything," he told us. I will call ahead so they are waiting for you upon arrival.

Our little girl's vocal cords were paralyzed in an open position, and we were told this was a regular sinus problem that was actually us pouring milk into her lungs instead of her stomach on a daily basis and constantly causing pneumonia. After a long battery of tests at Children's Hospital, they determined she had a malformation at the base of her brain called a Chiari malformation that was causing the paralysis, and it would require that they install a feeding tube and perform brain surgery on her to correct this birth defect.

I vividly remember sitting in the waiting room at the hospital, watching other families who had just handed off their children into the hands of doctors to fix problems with their children. The room was full of pain and hopelessness, but I remember being filled with a tremendous sense of peace that HE was full in control of our little girl and there would be nothing to worry about.

The next several months were filled with learning new ways to take care of our little baby. New ways to feed her and take care of the big scar on the back of her head. Our little 13-month-old girl continued to grow and develop normally, and now she is a perfect 30-year-old woman who bears no side effects from the crazy surgery except an extra belly button where the feeding tube was placed and a long nasty scar on her neck that is still covered by her beautiful strawberry-blonde hair.

Two times in my life when I felt totally helpless with the lives that I had been given to raise but never a time when I felt more at peace and in His perfect hands of protection. I now fully realize they always belonged to Him, and I was just blessed to have been given the chance to help raise them.

NOTES FROM DAD

Mark Hollander serves as executive director for Vision St. Charles County Leadership and spent 35 years in the banking business. Mark and his wife, Melissa, now own and operate La Belle Vie/The Café at Frenchtown. The café was recently honored as the "Best Breakfast Place in St. Louis" by *St. Louis Magazine* for 2023 and then "Small Business of the Year" by St. Charles Regional Chamber of Commerce for 2023.

Mark is a lifelong resident of St. Charles and has a passion for his community. He was also recently elected to serve on the City Council representing Ward 2.

Mark lives in St. Charles with his wife, Melissa, and their dogs — Stanley and Gibby. He enjoys spending time at their little lake cabin on Lake of the Ozarks and with his family. And, of course, watching Cardinals baseball.

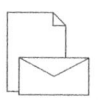

Clinton Schulte

The Bigger Song and Dance Plan

"Life's A Dance You Learn as you Go"
— **John Michael Montgomery**

This is the song I sing to my kids most nights. This song caught my attention in middle school when I could not find the courage to tell a girl I liked her. It has been true in every stage of life. Life is full of many unexpected twists and turns. I planned and planned and planned for what I wanted my life to be like. As a high school-aged young man, I had a plan for my career, and I had a plan for what my future wife, wedding, home, and family would look like. I knew I would marry a blonde, extroverted, and outgoing woman who loved to socialize and party as much as I did. We'd get married in the Catholic church I grew up in. I would never live in an apartment or condo. I would never live in a mobile home nor drive a compact car. I gripped the reins of life tightly, and nothing was going to buck me off the path I set out for myself. I knew who I was and who I was going to become. I could not have been more wrong!

It was April or May of my senior year of high school. I had no intention of going to college and planned to take over the family business of pouring concrete. It is just what you did in rural Missouri. I'm not sure how it happened, but I registered for college at Lindenwood University, where I was going to study criminal justice. I was going to be a police officer! Early in my time at LU, thanks to a Psych 101 course, I became obsessed with psychology and quickly changed my major to align with this newfound obsession. I never really understood why, but mental illness was interesting. I also wasn't fond of the idea of working with drug addicts. During these early college years, I was dumped by my girlfriend of over a year, which really didn't fit into my plans at all, nor did I see it coming. I would never have admitted it then, but I was in a lot of pain. I remember spending quite a bit of time crying. My new plan was to avoid any romantic relationship. A few weeks later, I entered a classroom with my future wife in the back row. I dropped that class, but fate still brought me to my wife just a couple of months later. After four years, I graduated and landed my first job working in a psychiatric hospital on a detox floor full of people struggling with drug addiction. At least I wasn't working with teenagers; they were terrifying!

At this time in my life, I was living life the way I thought it should be done. God wasn't anywhere on my radar. He was still there and at work, but I just didn't have my eyes open yet.

My future wife and I worked at the same hospital caring for patients struggling with mental illness and were planning on getting married. Through some research, I visited a potential site for our wedding. During this tour, I ran into some classmates from college who had started a treatment facility for teenage males struggling with drug addiction in a farm-like setting. They were looking for someone with a mental health background who could also run equipment, do construction, and care for farm animals. I was the perfect fit. Remember, I had life all planned out? I didn't want to work with teenagers or drug addicts and found myself being offered a position I was uniquely qualified for — working with teenagers who struggled with drug use.

During this time, we eloped and got married but hit struggles early on. We moved from our condo to a mobile home. I was ARROGANT and living life on my terms because I was the "man" of the house. Ultimately, I was an emotional mess. I felt like nothing was going well, and the rug had been ripped out from under me. I knew my wife loved me, but I wasn't sure she liked me anymore. I wasn't even sure I liked myself. Thankfully, I was surrounded by the right people to pick me up and reintroduce me to Jesus. I'm blessed that these men were there at the perfect time to pick me up. I thought I knew God because I had gone to Catholic school, and there was nothing more to learn. I knew that I had to start doing life differently, or I was going to contribute to the failed marriage statistics in the United States. I did not want to be in control of my life anymore, as if I was ever really in control. January 26, 2016, I handed Jesus the reigns for my life.

Jesus has the reigns, but that does not mean things will be happily ever after. It just means I trust God's plan for my life because He can see the whole plan. I am only able to see what is right in front of me. In March or April of that year, we were notified that we needed to move out of our mobile home. We were specifically told we needed to be gone in 28 days. I was panicked, but we were very fortunate to be able to move to my in-law's hunting trailer. We were just happy to have a place to go.

The hunting trailer was vacant most of the year and was a one-hour drive to both of our jobs. Because gas was expensive, we traded our truck for a compact car. This trailer was DIRTY! We cleaned it up the best we could, but it was still less than ideal. Due to the level of rodents we found when cleaning, we bought a dozen mouse traps to set the first night. As we lay in bed that night, we heard traps snapping all over. My foot even went through the bathroom floor one night when using the restroom. The craziest part of all of this horror story is I had never been happier in my life. We absolutely loved living there! To this day, my wife and I view this as an incredible experience and have nothing but gratitude for it.

You may ask yourself how we were so happy in a rodent-infested mobile home with a hole in the bathroom floor and only window air conditioners to keep it cool in the summer. My perspective had changed. No longer was I living my life based on my goals and objectives. My "plan," if it could even be called that, had fallen short in every way. Now, I was living my life on God's terms. I didn't, and still don't, know God's whole plan for my life, but I'm doing my best to live it with God at the center. Being a follower of Christ does not mean I am perfect — far from it. It means that through Christ, I become a better version of myself every day.

I want to recap where my life was at this point. As a self-proclaimed country boy, I was working in healthcare, wearing a button-up shirt, slacks, and dress shoes every day. I looked like I was getting dressed for homecoming every morning. I drove a compact car. I ended up receiving two graduate degrees. Who had I become? Remember that iron-clad plan I had? I did not plan on going to college, and I wasn't going to drive a compact car or live in a condo or mobile home. I was going to work in construction!

It is interesting now, looking back on all these plans that I had for my life. All my plans failed perfectly. They were all part of God's bigger plan for me. I am thankful every day that God did not answer those prayers or allow me to fulfill my own plan for my life.

What I hope you see in this story is my life turned out very differently than what I had dreamed! Every vision I set for my own life was not achieved. But, with every change of plan came growth. With every shortfall, I moved one step closer to the man I am today. Through the failure and challenges, I have learned and grown far more than I could have without the adversity in my life. Someone once told me that FAIL means

First Attempt In Learning. We are all living lives for the first time so give yourself, and others who make mistakes, the same level of grace as a baby learning to walk. I challenge you to embrace the challenges, embrace God's plan for your life, embrace failures, learn, and keep moving forward toward the person you are meant to become.

Clinton Schulte is a follower of Christ, a husband, and a father. He lives in St. Charles County, Missouri, where he works for a large healthcare system. Throughout his career, he has served in many industries, including retail, automotive, construction, mental health, and, finally, a broader healthcare industry through marketing. His personal and professional lives have taken many unexpected twists and turns to lead him to be the man he is today. Everything he has achieved so far can be credited to the Lord above, His plan, and the great people He put in Clinton's path to help me grow. His prayer is that the Lord uses him to bless others the way he has been blessed.

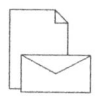

Dan Tripp

God, Money, Beer

Like other pre-teenage boys in the late 1980s, I would spend all my money at the arcade. This was still a time when you would take quarters to the arcade and line them up to compete against the winner. I guess this was the teenage version of playing pool in a bar. Instead of knocking in the eight ball, we were trying to knock out our competition in the game of Double Dragon. This two-person fighter game would take up hours of our time at the mall, where we would watch and learn the secret moves each player would have. Before the internet, you had to learn these secrets firsthand. Unfortunately, I was never really good at the game, and the older teenagers would beat me in seconds, and I would lose all my money.

In the spring of '88, Double Dragon was released on Nintendo NES. I knew if I could buy this game and practice at home, I would be able to perfect my moves and compete against the older kids. Unfortunately, I spent all of my allowance every week at the arcade, so I didn't have any money to buy the game that I knew would change my life. So, what does any pre-teen do when they don't have money? They ask Mom and Dad. The game was $50, and at the time, this was a pretty significant amount of money for a kid's game from my parents' point of view. They immediately said *no*, but I was persistent and said I would do whatever it took to earn this money. I told them I would do chores, clean the house, mow the lawn, wash their car, and even give the dog a bath. My dad wouldn't budge, but my mom gave in to my negotiating skills, and we came to an agreement that I would wash her car five times at $10 a wash. I guess she liked the idea of me working for my money and not just giving it to me.

After all, my parents were the hardest-working people I knew. They would always have two to three jobs. They would work all day long at their nine-to-five jobs, then would work at night at the local pizzeria. I guess this is the reason I have always wanted to open a brewery that serves pizza. The most important thing I learned from my dad is if you want something, you have to work for it.

On the other hand, my mom taught me another lesson that she didn't realize would later put me in debt and create a lifelong struggle with money. You see, I washed my mom's car and made that Buick Skylark look brand new again. As soon as I was finished, she drove me to Toys R Us to buy the game. After a few weeks, I lost interest in Double Dragon because it wasn't nearly as good as the arcade version, and I liked playing sports more than video games. To make matters worse, my mom never made me wash her car again.

This pattern continued, but not just with video games. If you ask my older brother and sister, they will tell you I would always get whatever I wanted (and I have to remind them this was because I was her favorite). After video games, it was skateboards, rollerblades, mountain bikes, and hockey equipment. Then after I turned 16, it was a motorcycle, cars, custom wheels, and computers. She taught me that all I needed to do was beg, bargain, plead, argue, or persuade, and when I promised I would do something in exchange, she never held me accountable. You see, my mom was a *GIVER*, and her love language was giving to others. She also taught me, though, that I could buy whatever I wanted even if I didn't have the money.

Fast forward another 16 years, and I started to see this pattern continue with my oldest son when he would spend time with his Nana. He would have this sense of entitlement and get whatever he wanted if all he did was beg, bargain, and plead. I get it; grandparents are supposed to spoil their grandkids, but at whose expense? My mom passed away from cancer, and my son was about the same age I was when my mom bought me that Double Dragon game. When we had to go through her estate, we realized she had tens of thousands in credit card debt, and most of the charges were for things she had bought for her kids and grandkids.

I didn't know him at the time, but Matt, my now business partner, and I were going to the same church together. His wife was battling cancer like my mom, and they both passed away about the same time. Through God's intervention, we ended up in the same Bible study and became friends. We both had the same passion for making beer. We started brewing beer together, and our combined family of 13 kids became friends. We would have monthly brew parties where we would invite our Bible study friends and others to brew beer and spend time together.

We became pretty good brewers and decided to open Good News Brewing Company. One of the hardest things was finding a commercial property that would allow us to brew beer and make wood-fired pizza. We were blessed to have other entrepreneurs believe in us and give us an opportunity. These entrepreneurs included Kevin and Tammy. They had recently purchased a laundromat that had a small office next to it; they were looking to lease it to a small business. We shared our story with them, and they said they loved what we are doing and believed in our vision and passion. They even said they would give us free rent until we opened if we did all of the construction and buildout.

For the next six months, we were at the brewery every weekend and day off. The best part about this was that our kids were right there with us. They helped demolish the ceiling, walls, and floors. The kids ripped pallet boards for decoration. They sanded, painted, and learned how to install drywall. They helped build the wood-fired pizza oven and basically learned how to start up a brewery. We didn't pay them. Instead, they learned what it takes to open a business. Now, after opening several locations, the kids are old enough and are working for us. Some weeks, they make more money than I do from my full-time teaching job. Some of our kids are assistant managers, some are managers, and some will someday be running the business for us.

One day, my youngest kids, who were not old enough to work for us, wanted me to buy them a trampoline. They begged, bargained, and pleaded that they "*needed*" a trampoline. Instead, I bought them an ice cream cart and their first supply of drumsticks, popsicles, and ice cream sandwiches. I told them that if they sold all of the ice cream to customers at the brewery, they would have enough money to buy that trampoline and more ice cream to continue their business. Now, every time any of my kids asks me to buy them something, I tell them to pick up shifts or sell some ice cream.

When my kids started making money, I wanted to teach them a different lesson than what my mom taught me. The first thing my wife and I did was deposit part of their checks into a savings account; we would never transfer more than half into their checking account.

By teaching our kids to live off half of their income, they have been able to save and invest. When they turned 15 and wanted to buy their own car, they had their own money. When they wanted to travel the country for a school trip, they were able to pay their own airfare. Sure, they have spent their money on stupid things like I did when I was a kid, but they are not spending borrowed money. By living debt-free, they are learning a lesson that will carry with them for the rest of their life and will be passed on for many generations.

When my mom passed away, and we received her life insurance, I would love to say that was the seed money for our business and investments, but we used it to pay off my debt instead. Someday, I will give our kids our estate, and I want to make sure they are not using it to pay off their bad debts.

Fathers, teach your children to walk humbly and fearfully with God. Proverbs 22:6 tells us: "Start children off on the way they should go, and even when they are old, they will not turn from it." This popular verse is written on many signs and shared by parents, but the next verse should also be included: "The rich rule over the poor, and the borrower is slave to the lender."

Elementary school should be an enjoyable part of your life. This was not the case for Dan Tripp. He struggled with reading, writing, and speech and was even held back a grade. When he found a passion for computer technology and wanted to enroll in a computer science program, he didn't have the academic background. He knew he had the passion and desire, but not the foundation and blamed his elementary teachers for not engaging him. He decided to devote his life to education and earned a bachelor's degree in elementary education and a master's and doctorate in educational leadership.

In addition, Dan was a part-time missionary for international and local ministries and was an avid home brewer. After serving almost two decades as an elementary teacher and administrator, he changed his passion to entrepreneurship and combined his faith and beer.

Dan and his business partner opened Good News Brewing Company in 2017 and have expanded to four locations and a coffee roasting company. His wife Annie and five kids have been important parts of the journey to help build and run the family business. Dan left elementary school but still has a passion for changing the educational system. Now, he teaches a high school entrepreneurship program, where he teaches his students how to start their own businesses, manage their money, and invest.

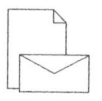

Jaime Morgan, LPC

Painful Lessons with My Son

It was just before 10 p.m. on a Thursday night when I turned to kiss my wife goodnight. It was part of our weekly ritual. Before you jump to conclusions about that ritual, my son has hockey practice at 6 a.m. every Friday, so we go to bed as early as we can on Thursdays. I'm up and ready by 5 a.m. on those mornings to hit the road. Friday is my only day off, but instead of sleeping in like most people would, I choose to invest that time in my son's future.

However, it wasn't always like this. I used to spend Friday mornings hungover from the night before, looking for someone to blame for the previous night's drunken mistakes. I used to wake up feeling sorry for myself and not even realizing it. I'd spend weekend after weekend looking to get into some trouble, doing things I knew I shouldn't be doing — I wasn't a model husband.

It's still hard to believe my life has changed so dramatically over the years. It's also hard to imagine that these early morning weekly pilgrimages will one day be a distant memory. Someday, I hope my son will look back on them fondly, as valuable time he spent with his old man.

Each week, my son and I reach uncharted territory in our conversations. We push ourselves to explore new ground in our morning dialogues, and we both learn something about ourselves in the process. Unlike talking with clients, speaking with my son is a time for me to learn.

I spend all week guiding and teaching, and while I learn a great deal from my clients daily, I am being paid to be the role of a mentor figure.

The innocence of children has a way of turning the tables on you and rearranging what you thought you knew about yourself. On these predawn drives, I am reminded by my 12-year-old son's inquisitiveness that I never had a father figure to teach me these lessons. Instead, I plunged forward without any paternal wisdom to guide me. As a result, I never learned how to treat people, how to truly care for a woman, or how to love and respect myself, for that matter. I only learned how to take the easy route. I learned the rest the hard way. I never thought I'd say it, much less write about it in a book, but staring at my son in the passenger seat, I'm grateful for every mistake I have ever made. If for no other reason, than so I can pass on the baton of fatherly wisdom and save him from making the same poor choices.

Today's drive is pretty silent. Static scenery shifts places. Trees bleed into green traffic lights, and shimmering neon signs for businesses that won't be open for another four hours glow in the predawn moonlight. I look at my son; he's engaged with a light-up screen. As I keep my eyes on the road, I feel a strong connection to Will. He's getting what I never had: a father to coach him, to love him, and to see him grow up and become a strong young man. I look back over and offer him a reassuring smile. His face lights up, this time not from his cell phone screen but from the trust and love we've built in our relationship.

Our gentle glances quickly swerve into deeper territory as he asks me a question that makes me nearly run us off the road. I take a deep breath and try to center myself. His words cut me a second time.

"Hey, Daddy, what made you have three divorces before Mama?"

"Oh, boy, that's a doozy, son," I think to myself, trying to find the right words and discernment to put this into context for my nearly 12-year-old son. Growing up in a world rife with social upheaval and change, I try to find something that will stick with him. I want him to have something he can take with him — even remember for the next 50 years — the kind of pep talk you see in the movies that I wish my father would have given me.

I take another big breath and say a silent prayer that my lips will find the right words. Still wet with my morning energy drink, my mouth begins formulating words.

"Son, your father was a victim."

"Like, someone robbed you?" Will's face wrinkles with worry.

"Not quite like that, Will. What I mean is that I felt like other people were always the bad guy. I felt like I was always getting hurt by the world. I had an attitude that made me feel like I was being wronged."

"Like a mindset?" he says, cocking his head sideways, still a little unsure of himself.

"Yeah, just like in hockey. My mindset was that I thought everyone else was wrong, and that I was right."

"You mean you blamed them? Is that what happened with Grandma?"

"That's right. I blamed Grandma for many years," I catch a glance of my eyes in the rearview.

"But why did you have three divorces — did you blame those on Grandma, too?"

"Partly. Will, when someone wants to be a victim, it doesn't matter what other people do or don't do. A victim will always find a reason to feel like it wasn't their fault. No matter what."

"But why would anybody want to be a victim? I don't understand, Daddy."

At this point, I could see the curiosity and the hope in his eyes, looking for a response that would make everything make sense.

"I don't know, Will. I really don't, and I can't undo the mistakes of the past. But what I can tell you is that I've learned. I learned that I don't want to be a victim. I want to be accountable for my actions, and I pray to God that you grow up to do better than your old man."

Will was silent for the next few minutes, letting my words sink in. I wondered what he was thinking — perhaps his own future and the lessons he would take from my life. The words I spoke felt like I was passing him a baton, not just of fatherly wisdom, but of my own missteps and the hard-earned lessons that he could choose to run with, or not.

In that silence, I felt the weight of my history — my flawed past and uncertain future — layered in my son's consciousness, just as surely as if I had filled him with the heartbreak and the strife that had marred my own life. But I also felt the weight of the possibility, of new beginnings, and of a future he could create for himself, unburdened by the chains of my own missteps.

My son will grow up in a world that is different from the one that shaped me — a world of smartphones and instant messages, a world that values transparency and accountability in a way that I never did. He will have the tools and the knowledge to face his life head-on, to acknowledge his own roles in his triumphs and tragedies, and to learn from the mistakes — my mistakes — so they will not define him.

He will have what I never did, and it will be because of the lessons that I share with him — ugly as they may be, painful as they surely will become. But if there is one thing I wish for my son, it is that he finds in my words the courage to shape his life and his relationships with an open heart and an open mind and that he learns not from his mistakes but from mine.

I love you, Will, and with every fiber of my being, I hope these words carve a path for a better future for both of us. Your old man is trying, for you and for the man he wishes to become, to become the wise father that I never had — the father I wish I had been.

The reality is that we will never have it "right," so as a dad, we have to show up every day and be the man we wish our own father was. We have to give our sons what we wish we would have had.

This is a condensed version of the last chapter of my book, "Master of Circumstance." It has been tailored for this project. I really hope you enjoyed it, and that this will make a difference in how you show up as a dad. You're important.

NOTES FROM DAD

Jamie Morgan is a licensed professional counselor with over ten years experience helping others break free from the constraints of circumstances to create a life they love. Author of "Master of Circumstance: Destroying the 7 illusions that keep you from living life intentionally" his podcast, "Master of Circumstance" encourages listeners to break free from a victim mindset, take control of their circumstances, and make conscious choices that will bring greater joy into their lives.

Jamie believes everyone has the ability to live a life full of meaning and fulfillment and is passionate about creating a life with purpose, intentionality, and joy. Offering workshops and online courses that provide practical advice on reclaiming control over one's life, Jamie is committed to helping people live an intentional life and embrace the power of choice.

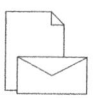

John Whitehead

Can I Go With You?

Becoming a father has been, and will always be, the best thing to ever happen to me. You could almost say, "My heart needed it." Yes, there are days you will be overwhelmed, overstimulated, frustrated, and downright exhausted, but I'll be damned if, two minutes after bedtime, I don't miss those kids and want them right back in my arms.

My oldest, Colton and I are inseparable. To the point now where I can feel my wife's eyes rolling whenever he says, "Can I go with you?" That kid wants to be with and around dad 24/7. He's a self-proclaimed daddy's boy and will give me "knucks" and likes to say, "Just the boys." Every time I leave the house, he puts his shoes on and expects to go with me, and that means the world to me. It could be anything from going to the grocery store or closing down the coffee shop for the night. This is not lost on me, and it makes me feel like I am the richest man in the world.

Now, let's come back down to reality for a second. While being a dad Is fun, think about how big a responsibility it is. There's a lot more to raising children than just keeping them hydrated and fed. I look back and try to remember what my expectations were. Dads are supposed to provide for their family. Dads are supposed to be strong. Dads are supposed to have the ever-flowing energy to play. Dads are supposed to be the shining light in a dark room. A dad fights off the monsters. Is the calming presence in a chaotic situation. Dads are supposed to be their coach, mentor, leader, and, ultimately, their hero. The real question here is what am I doing to make sure I hit these expectations? There are times when I struggle and believe I don't deserve the love, attention, and accolades that my children give me.

I can explain what a child wants in five simple words: SHOW UP AND BE PRESENT. You do this, and you will be their hero. You may not be strong like the Hulk, rich like Iron Man, as cool as Thor, or as perfect as Captain America. But what you are is tangible. What you are is real. The hero they need. Never forget this. It doesn't matter if you don't make enough money, are overweight, aren't handy, or whatever other excuse you can throw around. Show up for them. Be present for them, and I'd bet you're doing just fine in their book. Some Ideas:

- Put the phone down.
- Ask them about their day and be engaged in the conversation.
- Say yes when they ask you to play with them — no matter how tired you are.
- Always keep your word and the promises you make them.
- Remind them often that you are proud of them and that they are doing great.
- Be the man your kids think you are.
- Never stop showing or telling them that they are loved.

"Be the man your kids think you are." This has played in my head for as long as I can remember. It's a heavy gut punch. Not necessarily in a bad way, but in a way that reminds you reality is here. It's not next month; it doesn't "start on Monday." It's here and offers examples and OPPORTU-NITIES to show your children how to be their best selves.

Colton: "Remind them often that you are proud of them and that they are doing great."

One of the neatest interactions between my oldest son and me happened just this morning. This morning, it was just me and Colton. My wife was taking "the littles" (middle child, Dean, and youngest, Kinley) to daycare. As I stated earlier, he is a daddy's boy and loves when it's the two of us — him watching his Pokémon shows and telling me all about it. As we approached his school, tornado sirens began sounding. He was in his own world and unfazed.

"Hey buddy, I need you to put the iPad down and listen to me." He sighed but did it.

"Do you hear that sound? Do you know what that is for?" This takes him a few seconds, but he nodded his head and begins to tear up. He started talking about how he doesn't like tornadoes and storms. I asked if he remembers what they practiced in school, and we talked about how the school is much safer than the truck.

As we pulled in the lot, he can tell things are a bit off. Cars are moving a little faster, adults and teachers waving their hands at cars, signaling the children to get inside — what seems like an army of kids running from their cars and into the school. I pulled up to our drop-off point and looked back to hug him. He put his forehead down on mine and said, "Daddy, I got this."

He put his hood up on his jacket, hopped out of the truck, and ran into school. Who do you think was the one tearing up now? The sense of pride, happiness, worry, and pure love was overwhelming, and I couldn't do anything but smile. He just became the little man that I needed, but more importantly, that HE needed himself to be. I'm proud of you Colton, and you are doing great!

Dean: "Be the man your kids think you are."

Dean is an absolute firecracker (his daddy to a T). Dean is funny, clever, absolutely fearless, hardheaded, and one of the toughest kids you will ever meet. I often joke that if I could only pick one person to have with me to walk down a dark alley with, then I'd take my 3-year-old Dean. His confidence is unmatched. Having said that, he is the sweetest, most caring individual who puts others first (he ALWAYS looks out for his siblings). He is my independent one. Always asking questions, always watching your every movement, and then mimicking. But really what he's doing is trying to articulate and understand how to do things, how he can do certain things, and how to act in situations.

In our household, we preach that ladies come first, that our responsibility is to treat everyone, but especially mom and sissy, with the utmost respect and care. One afternoon, our youngest was napping, my oldest and I were playing soccer in the driveway, and Dean was sitting on the front porch with Jen in our white rocking chairs, enjoying a sunny day in early spring. Jen looked at him and said, "Deaners, are you going to take care of Momma forever?" He turned to her, smiled, and said, "I'll fight the bad guys, too." The sense of pride I felt when hearing Jen sharing this moment with me is unexplainable.

We all grow up wanting to be a superhero, and, as parents, we tell our kids not to worry about the dark, the monsters under the bed, or any other weird scenario they tell you about during their chicken nugget dinner. But, men, understand this: He could have said no. He could have joked like he always does and simply said, "Yes, Momma". However, he chose not to. He knew to SHOW UP AND BE PRESENT for his Momma, and I believe it to be because he is a product of his surroundings. "Be the man your kids think you are" because they WILL follow.

Kinley: "Never stop showing or telling them they are loved."

Being wrapped around her finger is an understatement. I always wanted to experience having both a son and a daughter. I never could have guessed or been prepared for how much joy this little girl brings me.

She's at that amazing age where she's still so young and cuddly but also starting to show you who she is as a person. She's needy, independent, smart, and sassy. She plays both sides, too. She can be an absolute Daddy's girl, but she always turns right back around and shows all that attention to Mom, too.

The experience that sticks out the most is one random car ride. Dean, looking out the window, drinking his juice, Colton in the middle seat and in his own world playing his Nintendo Switch. The car was silent for a moment as we had just finished jamming out to "London Bridge" by Fergie (Dean's request). Out of nowhere, I hear, "Dada, Luh you." Now, I know kids say the darnedest things and that being random is typically normal. I choose to believe she chose that moment in the calm to say it for a few reasons. She felt happy, she felt safe, she felt calm, and more important, she felt comfortable. "Never stop showing or telling them they are loved." It is exactly what they need.

Isn't that what we want for our kids? The sense that the world is a perfect place because I am with the people I love the most. I choose to believe she feels this because she has someone who is extremely involved, someone who will wrestle her, cuddle on the couch, run my hands through her hair while she relaxes, and drinks juice on my chest. And because she has someone she believes in. Someone who SHOWS UP AND IS PRESENT.

At the end of the day, I need to get better and be better for them. As they grow, so should we. One new thing I started, and I know a lot of other people do this, too, is create email accounts for the kids. I take so many pictures of them that I barely have the storage on my phone, and we keep these for memories, right? So now, and similar to the title of this book, I will email the kids pictures from the weekend, the occasion, or even the random interactions at home and leave them a nice little "*Note from Dad.*"

John Whitehead was born and raised in St. Louis. He is a graduate of Benedictine College in Atchison, Kan, where he earned a bachelor's degree in business management and marketing. Married to his beautiful wife, Jennifer, in 2014, John is a father of three amazing children: Colton, Dean, and Kinley. An entrepreneur at heart, John has worked as a consultant with Farmers Insurance group since 2015 and recently in 2022 opened a coffee franchise (PJ's Coffee) in the O'Fallon, Mo area with his family. When not in business mode, you'll find John playing, watching, or talking all things hockey (Go BLUES!) and, of course, being a DAD!

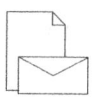

Lance Rogers

What's Your Story?

Everyone reading this chapter has their own story. I would guess very few of our stories are perfect. I, however, felt like I was living a fairytale until one fateful Friday evening. I remember this date like it was yesterday… June 13, 1975.

My brother and I were born into a loving family. Our parents met in college, and their love story began there. They loved each other dearly. Our dad was hard-working and well-respected in the community. Our mother worked as a teacher. She loved her children, always putting us before herself. We were a perfect family from the outside looking in, or in pictures. We had a really good life. Our dad spent time with us. We fished. We hunted. We played sports. He coached. He was a banker and good with people. He was involved in the community and well thought of. There was no place he went in or outside of town where someone did not know him. We went wherever he went. We did not do anything we could not all do together. He was always there until that fatal Friday. Our lives changed forever that night.

Our dad was my hero. I looked up to him immensely. I wanted to be just like him. Our dad was perfect, and there was not anything that he could not do or conquer. Or, so I thought. Little did we know our dad suffered from depression. This mental illness took his life. He committed suicide at 38, leaving our mother a widow at 36 with two boys (10 and 6 years old) to raise on her own on a teacher's salary. Depression or any type of mental illness was taboo back then. You did not talk about it. You did not mention it. You dealt with it and were left to figure it out on your own, with your own demons and devices. Plus, the way our dad died was a metaphorical "Scarlet Letter" to our mother and our family. You dealt with this "Scarlet Letter" the same way depression was handled back then. Suicide was taboo. You did not talk about it. You did not mention it. You dealt with it and were left to figure it out on your own. With your own demons and devices.

I share this with you now because three years ago, I could not, would not, nor would I have even given it a thought. It was my guilt. It was my shame. It was my baggage. It was my past. It was mine to keep buried. Hidden so no one could ever see my "Scarlet Letter." I thought my dad committed suicide because of something I did or did not do. I was sad. I was anxious. I was lost. I was scared. I was angry. I was numb. I was in despair. I was in pain. Life was hard. At times, life was more than I could bear. I struggled with my worth. No one knew. I buried it all and kept moving forward, challenging and driving myself toward goals. I thought these accomplishments would finish life for my dad and make him proud of me. Then I turned 39. What do I do now?

I was wayward for so many years. It took me more than 40 years to figure out that it was not my fault and there was nothing I could have done to prevent our dad's depression, or his death. This is the journey that led me to one important realization. I may have grown up without a dad, but I ALWAYS had a Father in heaven. A Heavenly Father who ALWAYS loved me. A Heavenly Father who was ALWAYS with me. A Heavenly Father who protected me. And this was despite myself, in spite of my doubts, in spite of my fears, in spite of my weakness, despite my failures, and despite all my sins.

Our Heavenly Father is with each of us through our joy and sorrow, through life's peace and storms. This revelation has changed everything for me. It has made me want to be a better man, a better husband, a better father, a better brother, a better friend, a better steward, a better worker, a better teammate, a better person. This change has only been possible because God has been the reason and at the center of this transformation.

So, this is where "Notes From Dad" begins for my children. I have often tried to jot thoughts down in a journal for you, thinking that one day I would make them into a printed copy for each of you. I have to be honest, though; I usually forget my thoughts before I get the chance to write them down. The journaling is few and far between. These thoughts are not so much the things I have done right but all the things I have done wrong or learned from. My children, I want you to know you are the best of me. You are what I did right (and marrying your mother). I cannot even begin to tell you what each of you means to me, how proud I am of who you are, and how much I love each of you. Being your dad is one of the most wonderful blessings and priceless gifts I am most grateful for. It is hard for me to write these words without tears in my eyes.

This is for you and your children and your children's children and their children for generations to come. My experience for where you should keep your focus:

- God
- Family
- Work
- Always be kind.
- Be empathetic.
- Social intelligence does not need an IQ test.
- Do not be afraid to break cycles.
- Two roads diverge; do not be afraid to take your own path.

- Do not be afraid to make a tough decision when it is the right thing to do.
- Be strong and courageous and know you may be by yourself, but you are never alone.
- It is OK to be strong willed, not stiff-necked.
- Your past does not define you or your future.
- Your failures do not define you or your future, either.
- You may reap what you sow, but don't forget that you have to plow before you plant and water.
- Show up. Work hard. Do the work. Do your best. With a good attitude.
- Showing up is 50 percent of everything. Attitude is the other 90 percent. (OK, this is my own Yogi-ism).
- Talk is cheap. Actions speak.
- Display honesty and integrity in everything you do and say.
- Always be genuine and sincere.
- Shaking a person's hand, looking them in the eyes, and listening to what they have to say are still standards to live by.
- Do not be afraid to stand firm when you know you are right or in the right.
- More important, do right.
- Perseverance. Do not ever give up!
- Build a firm foundation, not a house of cards.
- Remember your heritage and your family that came before you. The sacrifices they made and the lives they lived are the opportunities you have today.
- Be grateful, always.
- Do not be afraid to be a parent. Discipline your children.

- Life will never be fair. Put your faith and hope in Jesus.
- Pray. And pray some more.
- Know your strength comes from the Lord God Almighty.
- God is the source of wisdom. Honor Him and apply this knowledge.
- Remember, nothing in this world or of this world is perfect. There is only a perfect God.
- Make and keep God the center of your marriage, your family, and your work.
- God provides everything and is in everything. Seek Him. Pursue Him. He is always there, even in the quiet.

Not only is this chapter a note to my children, but it is also a chapter for those boys and girls, those sons and daughters who grew up without a dad. It is for those dads who are struggling. This chapter is even for widows or single mothers trying so hard to make up for the dad who may not be present in the home. Know you have a Heavenly Father who loves you beyond measure and is with you ALWAYS.

"Have I not commanded you? Be strong and courageous; do not be afraid, nor be dismayed, for the Lord your God is with you wherever you go." – **Joshua 1:9 NKJV.**

My warmest and deepest wish for those who read these chapters is to know that you are not alone and that there is hope and comfort for wherever you may be in life's journey, whatever personal battles or storms you may be facing and wrestling with. This is only a short chapter of what our Heavenly Father has in store for each of you!

What's the rest of your story?

Lance Rogers was born and raised in north-central Missouri. The oldest of two brothers, his parents and grandparents instilled strong values and a strong work ethic in him. He worked a full-time job and several others to put himself through college, graduating from Truman State University in Kirksville, MO.

His career has been in sales and operations management, directing and developing teams to execute and deliver results. Lance has a passion for mentoring and teaching. He also has a passion for serving his church and community. Lance has been married to his wife, Lisa, since 1991. They have three adult children who are married and starting families of their own. They are grandparents with many more grandchildren to follow.

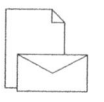

Bob Kolf

Only Jesus Can Save the World

"Grandpa, only Jesus can save the world."

These are the words told to me by one of my granddaughters when I asked her what she was going to be when she grew up. When she didn't answer me right away, I said, "I'll bet you are going to grow up one day to save the world." I was astonished by her answer. She was only ten years old. Ever since she corrected me, I no longer proclaim that my life's purpose is to save the world, but rather, it is to make our community in St. Louis stronger and more vibrant. She was right; only Jesus can save the world. All that a mere mortal like me can do is to do my small part to help build God's kingdom here on earth.

I was born in 1955 in Milwaukee. My dad was a computer programmer. He was my mentor and role model. He was also a disciplinarian and the spiritual leader of the family. He often kept us in stitches with his dry sense of humor. "Nuts to you," he would always say as he started the bowl of nuts around the dinner table after the cake was served at a family member's birthday. My conservative, religious, and family values come from him.

My mom was the primary caregiver and nurturer for me and my eight siblings. After my youngest sister was old enough to be left on her own, my mom returned to work as a social worker. My ability and desire to nurture and care for people come from her. God truly blessed me with very loving and caring parents and a large and strong family unit. My parents taught me how to share and the importance of treating others the way that I wanted to be treated.

I was raised in the Catholic Church. I always wanted to become a priest. I felt that this was my calling from God. My dad, too, had wanted to become a priest, but because he had juvenile diabetes, his mom discouraged him from pursuing that dream of his for fear he might have an insulin reaction while on the altar of the Lord. I attended the diocesan prep seminary in Milwaukee during my freshman year in high school. During that time, I discerned that the priesthood was something I could not commit to.

I was always good at math and science. I was told during my junior year at Marquette University High School that my purpose in life was to become an engineer. As I had no reason to question this logic, I headed off to the University of Arkansas in 1973 to pursue a degree in civil engineering. My favorite professor told me that when I graduated, I would have three job offers, work 40 years, and retire. It all went according to God's plan. I spent those 40 years in Arkansas, Texas, Oklahoma, Georgia, and Missouri, where my wife and I moved to in 1985.

My beautiful and loving wife, Vicki, and I met at the University of Arkansas. She was my assigned "little sister" from the sorority that my fraternity socialized with. I broke the cardinal rule that said you must not, under any circumstances, date your little sister. Somehow, we never got called out on that. We have been married for 43 years and have raised three beautiful and loving daughters, all of whom became Registered Nurses. We also have three wonderful sons-in-law and eight beautiful grandchildren. As of this writing, we have one more grandchild on the way. The challenge in life is to keep a good work-life balance and keep your priorities straight. We have always kept God first, our children and family a close second, followed by our careers, and then everything else.

I retired in 2017 after 40 years as a civil/structural engineer. It was a financially rewarding and challenging career, and I have been responsible for several hundred commercial and industrial building structures. I can tell you, however, that I now sleep much better at night because I don't have structural calculations swirling in my head at 2:00 in the morning while attempting to go to sleep. My advice is to celebrate your many accomplishments, or those one or two bad mistakes you made along the way will remain to haunt you.

Upon retirement, I wanted to work, albeit in something completely different. For the first 40 years of my working career, I pursued the analytical half of my brain, which I inherited from my dad, the computer programmer. For the next 40 years, I want to do something to help others, just like my mom, the social worker.

I found a new purpose in my life on the day the world ended in March 2020. Working for RockIt Careers in Chesterfield at the time, I was sent home as we were all told that we were "nonessentials." I went home. I thought this was no way to spend retirement, isolated from the rest of the world. During lockdown, it was a ghost town. I missed interacting with other human beings outside of my inner circle.

Using my introverted self, I started connecting on LinkedIn with the approximate 200,000 workers in the Greater St. Louis region who lost employment in March and April. I would type in "Greater St. Louis" and "Pandemic." A bazillion profiles popped up on my computer screen. They all said the same thing, "Laid off due to Pandemic." I connected with as many job seekers as I could. Enterprise and Maritz were two of the companies who had massive layoffs due to the shutdown of the travel and hospitality industries. After the first week, I had 200 new connections.

I asked them to join a group I was starting that would come to be called "Job Seekers' Garden Club of St. Louis," so named because we do for job seekers what gardeners do for plants. We care for them, nurture them, and help them grow in their careers.

After building my base of job seekers, it was time to add recruiters. By September 2020, the LinkedIn group had swelled to more than 1,000. I had a job seeker who joined the group. She did not have a resume and asked if she could simply post a referral letter from her employer, who laid her off. I said, "Sure, what the heck, let's give it a try." She posted. I tagged three recruiters. She got seven phone calls that day and was hired in 15 hours. I knew then that the group I had started using my problem-solving skills as a structural engineer and divine inspiration from the Holy Spirit was something special. The group is now more than 5,400 strong and is a 501(c)(3) nonprofit, helping countless hundreds of job seekers find their new life's purpose.

The world is a whole lot different than the one I grew up in during the 1960s and 1970s. There were no cell phones back then. There was no internet. Nobody worked on Sundays except for essential workers. We ate dinner together as a family. We went to church together, studied, and prayed together. I remember a couple of times when the entire family of 11 would pile into the family station wagon to go apple picking out in the countryside on a Sunday afternoon. We all had chores. We showed respect to our parents. Yes, we occasionally fought like siblings do, but for the most part, we got along together.

This is not the world we live in today. Social media has had a dramatic impact on our lives. It can be a good thing, but quite often, it can be a very bad thing as well. It can be a source of isolation and can lead to fear, depression, anxiety, and even suicide. Teaching our children and grandchildren limits, helping them to discern between right and wrong, and keeping an open dialogue with them are more important now than ever.

I want my children and grandchildren to know that we have an incredibly strong and vibrant multicultural community in St. Louis. I pray that they stay close to God, discover their God-given talents, and match their talents with their passions to discover God's purpose in their lives. I pray that they learn to love their neighbors. I hope that they will express gratitude for what they are given and show compassion and generosity to those in need.

I believe that Jesus died on the cross to redeem our sins. It is up to each one of us to accept His gift of salvation by living our lives according to His commandments. This is what I want my children and grandchildren to know.

Here is my closing prayer, an excerpt from the prayer of St. Francis:

> "O divine Master, grant that I may not so much seek to be consoled as to console, to be understood as to understand, to be loved as to love. For it is in giving that we receive, it is in pardoning that we are pardoned, and it is in dying that we are born to eternal life."

NOTES FROM DAD

Bob Kolf is a husband, a father of three, and a grandfather of eight-plus. He is the founder and executive director of Job Seekers' Garden Club of St. Louis (JSGCSTL.org). He is a parishioner at Ascension Catholic Church in Chesterfield, MO. where he and his wife, Vicki, are members of the Society of St. Vincent de Paul, serving those most in need in our community. He can be reached on LinkedIn.

Bob's journey through life has had its many ups and downs, its trials and tribulations. During the darkest hours of his life, such as when his parents died and when extremely difficult situations arose during his working career, he always turned to God. He has also had a very supportive family to turn to, for which he is full of gratitude. The most important thing that Bob's dad told him was, "Always count your blessings." Bob counts Dad and Mom as his heroes.

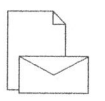

Joel Mikos

Silent Heart: A Father's Message to His Son

On August 31, 2000, I awoke exhausted and groggy but ready to begin my day. I was more tired than usual, but I had been burning the candle at both ends for some time. I let the dog out, stretched, and made some coffee, but I felt "off" somehow.

As I ate breakfast and went through my routine, I noticed my phone was acting up and looked like the time when I accidentally changed my language settings on my phone to something unrecognizable. I thought, "Oh well, I'll have to search for how to change it back when I get to work."

I showered, shaved, and got ready. Traveling to work, I listened to my favorite song, "Restless Love" by Cory Asbury, and looked at my car, trying to figure out why it sounded so "off." The lyrics were wrong, the song was out of tune, and the words were in another language.

Fast-forward 48 hours, and I was in a hospital. The doctor came in and said, "You've had a stroke. Two strokes, to be exact, and if you have another, that's it for you."

Talk about a pep talk! I asked if there was anything else, maybe some good news. She said, "I'm concerned you're not taking this seriously!" I acknowledged her and let her know that it doesn't help to get upset.

For the previous two days, I was working on recognizing symbols, letters, and shapes all over again. My brain had suffered two strokes. Someone, somewhere, decided, "You need to pull it together." I had to rest and allow my brain to heal. Luckily, everything came back; some things went fast, and some things went slow.

I was given a second chance, and within two days, I was talking when I couldn't speak well before. Texting when I couldn't spell. It was as if someone had told me, "You need to refocus!" After this happened, I was looking for answers, but medicine had little to go on.

I asked the doctor, "How did this happen?" She said, "I can't explain it. Every test we have shows you're healthy, minus the two parts of your brain that are gone and will never come back. To put it more in perspective, the next youngest patient here in the stroke wing is in their 70s. You are the youngest stroke patient here."

I realized this was a sign. Not only that, but this happened on my sister's birthday. She would be used to a belated birthday card, but not this news. And this was during the pandemic on top of it.

I tell you all of this, son because I'm not sure how I would teach you everything I have to teach you without speech, without reading to you, without writing or texting to you.

What I do have is motivation. I am not perfect. I fall, I get back up. I have emotions, and I can be impatient. I work hard, but I can always work harder. Let me take some time while I still can to share with you what I have learned, what my father has taught me, and what his father taught him.

You are surrounded by people, and people are good until proven otherwise. Some have been fortunate, and some have been unfortunate. Some are just scraping by using the only tools they have to survive. Some were born with God-given talent that launches them into success. Some spend thousands of hours working on skills that don't lead them to any success at all. You can do everything right and still fail. Recognize the talents you were born with and realize that skills are to be developed.

Every person in life has a purpose. For fathers, I would love that purpose to be their children and their family, but as men, we get distracted. When you decide what you want to do, go for it! Listen to no one but your heart, and do what you were meant to do. Your purpose is what keeps you away from distractions.

That being said, find a partner who is your best friend, the love of your life, and the mother of your children. These are the three things that helped me fall madly in love with your mother. She is one of a kind.

There's nothing that touches my heart more than when someone says to me, "I love your wife." It fills my soul and makes my eyes well up. Do everything you can to appreciate your partner. She is the strongest, bravest, happiest, and most beautiful person I have ever met. All I want for you is someone who makes you feel the same. I will warn you, it is hard work being a man. As a husband and father, I fall lovingly so I can pick myself up again and learn to create another skill. As men, our failures give us a chance to learn, to examine it, and to create a way to build a new strength. It is the weakest of men that never admits that he's failed, that he's vulnerable.

Surround yourself with good people. Build them up, and they will build you up. I was born and raised in a cynical world and society, and what I've learned most is that people break you down because you threaten them or because they can only build themselves up by breaking others down. I've fallen into this trap; it's fruitless.

Don't be a bully. Hurt people, hurt people. Stand up for yourself and others, but don't break others down. I'm blessed because you have a heart bigger than I could ever imagine.

Thank you for being who you are, and thank God you are a gentle soul. There's an old saying, "Show me your friends, and I'll show you your future." This is true. I've been blessed to be surrounded by some of the best individuals — men, fathers, brothers —to have met with and had discussions with. Any one of them would have Dad's notes to offer that would be profound.

Read. Read more and more every day. The more you read, the better you will be. At some point in the future, I hope to read more and more, and as I get older, to become older and wiser. Maybe even to be the wise and "honest man" that the philosopher Diogenes was looking for with his lamp. Regardless, not everyone absorbs the written word.

Social media is great for connecting and promoting ideas and individuals. Nothing will replace the written word. No one can replace face-to-face contact.

Save your money. Save as much and as often as you can. I have not been perfect with this, but I can tell you that George S. Clason's book "*The Richest Man in Babylon*" is the greatest short read on the why and how of saving for the future.

Take care of your body. It is a temple that was given to us. I remember having so much fun at the store, watching you discover the difference between sugar, fat, and carbohydrates. When it comes to food, there is no substitute for quality. As time has gone on, food quality has declined. Everyone's diet is different. There are fads out there. What works best are the habits you have developed that grow your body and help your mind focus. The healthiest cells are built from the healthiest sources of food. There are no shortcuts. Know that as a fact and memorize it!

Drugs. No. Which ones are OK? Let me put it this way: do everything possible to stay away from all drugs. Eliminate the need for pharmaceuticals. Every cell in your body survived without the need for drugs.

Remember, healthy people don't get sick. The healthier your body is, the faster your recovery from illness, injury, and disease. Unhealthy people become so because of unhealthy habits. While I don't know why I was hospitalized, I know my recovery had much to do with previous habits that were ingrained early. Genetics are outside of our control. This does happen. Stay healthy. Share what you know works for you with others and be passionate about taking care of yourself.

Respect is always given before it is received. The only thing you can control in life is understanding others and what they are willing to receive in terms of language and communication. Do your best to honor and respect them. Grow thicker skin and allow people more latitude to communicate their true feelings to you. They will appreciate you for it. If everyone did this and took the time to understand one another, there would be less conflict. We could use a world with less violence and more understanding.

Be on time. I have struggled with this, but it has always benefited me more in life to be early. I never got the break that I deserved when I was late. Life is simpler when you understand this. Early is on time, and on time is late. Late is still late.

I hope this helps you through your years. I hope it guides you, and I hope I keep my mind sharp, my heart pure, and my speech clear in the years to come.

I love you, son, whether I can say it or not.

NOTES FROM DAD

Dr. Joel Mikos, born in the Chicagoland area and raised in Tinley Park, IL, is a passionate chiropractor with over 25 years of experience in the field. Born to a mother who dedicated over 50 years to her work as an x-ray/mammogram technician. His father, a U.S. Army veteran, who spent five decades as a business owner, painter and decorator, Joel learned the value of hard work and dedication from an early age.

After relocating to Chesterfield, MO to pursue his education at Logan University, Joel fell in love with the St. Louis area and decided to make it his home. Graduating with a B.S. in Human Biology and his Chiropractic degree, Joel became an instructor and director at a local St. Louis College, teaching over 5,000 hours in the classroom.

Outside of his professional life, Joel enjoys spending quality time with his wife Salena, and son Adrian; traveling, playing sports, and indulging in a good meal. His dedication to helping his community achieve and maintain optimal health is unwavering, making him a respected and beloved figure in the world of chiropractic care..

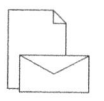

Tim Ruyle

Principles for a Life Fulfilled

Faith

My greatest desire is to impart wisdom and guidance to my children, with the hope that I can inspire them as they journey through life. Among the most precious gifts I can offer is an understanding of the significance of faith and its profound impact on the family unit.

Christian faith is more than a set of beliefs; it is, in my humble opinion, the cornerstone of the family's values, guiding our thoughts, words, and actions. At its core, Christianity teaches us to love God above all else and to love our neighbors as ourselves. This fundamental principle forms the foundation of how we conduct ourselves, whether in the privacy of our homes or when we are interacting with the rest of the world.

In a world filled with uncertainty and turmoil, our faith provides us with a sense of stability and hope. We find comfort in knowing that we are never alone and that our God stands beside us through every trial and tribulation. Our faith teaches us to trust in God's plan, even when we cannot see the way forward, knowing that His love and grace will sustain us through the darkest times.

Our faith also serves as a source of strength and resilience, equipping us to face life's challenges with courage and grace. When we encounter obstacles or setbacks, we turn to God in prayer, seeking His guidance and wisdom. Through our faith, we find the strength to persevere, to rise above adversity, and to emerge stronger and more resilient than before.

Perhaps, most important, our faith binds us as a family, uniting us in love, purpose, and shared values. That faith provides us with a common foundation upon which to build our relationships, fostering a sense of belonging and mutual respect. As we gather together for prayer, worship, and fellowship, we strengthen the bonds that tie us together, while also humbling ourselves in our belief that God is in control, and we should trust in His love for us.

I can speak from experience that your faith will be challenged many times throughout your life. My faith is tested every time I see bad things happen to good people. We often blame God for "allowing" this to happen. But what we can't see is the divine plan that includes many events that span the spectrum of good to bad. These events are woven together to form His plan for the world and we aren't meant to understand it.

As you grow and mature, I hope you will come to see the value and purpose of the Christian faith, not only for your personal growth and fulfillment but also for the strength and vitality of our family unit. May it be a beacon of light in times of darkness, a source of comfort in times of need, and a guiding star that leads you ever closer to God's love and grace.

Family

I am compelled to share one of the most profound lessons life is still teaching me, a lesson about the importance of family and the role of suffering as it shapes us within the family and in our Christian faith.

First and foremost, I want you to understand the paramount significance of family. The family unit is not just a collection of individuals bound by blood; it is a sacred institution — a sanctuary of love, support, and belonging. In a world that is often chaotic, illogical, misguided, and uncertain, the family stands as a steadfast anchor, providing us with a sense of security and purpose. It's sometime the only place where you find serenity, logic, guidance, and certainty.

Family is where we find comfort in times of sorrow, celebrate each other's triumphs, and share life's most precious moments. It is where we learn the values of kindness, compassion, and forgiveness — virtues that form the foundation of our character and shape the course of our lives. My family is my greatest treasure, a source of joy and strength that enriches my journey through this world.

But alongside the joys of family life, there inevitably are moments of hardship and suffering. As Christians, we are not exempt from the trials and tribulations of life; rather, we are called to embrace them as an integral part of our journey of faith.

Suffering, though difficult to endure, plays a crucial role in our spiritual growth and development. It is through our experiences of suffering that we learn to lean on God's strength and grace, trusting in His providence even when the path ahead seems uncertain. Suffering teaches us humility, reminding us of our dependence on God and our need for His mercy and guidance. While it may sound counterintuitive, it is because God loves us that he expects us to suffer.

But perhaps most important, suffering offers an opportunity to strengthen our family relationships while drawing us closer to God in our times of greatest need. It is during moments of suffering that we discover the true depth of love we have within the family unit — a love that transcends our pain and suffering, offering us hope, healing, and redemption.

As you navigate through life, remember that family is a beacon of light in the darkness — a source of love, strength, and support that will carry us through even the darkest of times. When you inevitably encounter suffering along the way, embrace it as an opportunity to cling tighter to your family and to grow in your faith, trusting in that family's unfailing love and in God's grace to sustain you through that time of suffering.

Freedom

Finally, it is my duty as a patriot to share with you the importance of freedom, drawing inspiration from the brave souls who forged our nation founded on the principles of liberty and justice for all and for all of those who sacrificed so much to preserve that freedom for nearly 250 years.

America's founding fathers were men of vision and courage who dared to dream of a world where freedom reigned supreme. They understood that true freedom is not merely the absence of oppression but the presence of opportunity — the opportunity to pursue our dreams, speak our minds, and "Secure the Blessings of Liberty."

The First Amendment of the United States Constitution guarantees us the freedom of speech, religion, press, assembly, and petition. These rights are the bedrock of our democracy, allowing us to express ourselves freely, worship as we choose, and hold our government accountable to the people it serves. They remind us that freedom is not a gift bestowed upon us by benevolent rulers but a birthright that we must cherish and defend at all costs.

The Second Amendment, often referred to as the right to bear arms, is a testament to the importance of self-defense and individual liberty. Our founding fathers understood that a well-armed populace is essential to safeguard against tyranny and oppression. They recognized that the right to bear arms is not only a means of protecting ourselves and our families but also a symbol of our inherent right to freedom and self-determination.

The Fourth Amendment protects us against unreasonable searches and seizures, ensuring that our privacy and personal property are safeguarded from government intrusion. It reminds us that freedom means more than just the absence of physical restraints; it means having the autonomy to live our lives free from unwarranted surveillance and interference.

But freedom is not just a political concept; it is a way of life — a mindset that transcends borders and boundaries. It is the freedom to innovate, create, explore new frontiers, create value, and exchange value for value. You may have heard it said that "money is the root of all evil"; however, that's not true. In fact, "The *love* of money is the root of all evil." This truth is more evident today than it's ever been. To be free, we must be free of the incentives that motivate us to *love* money. For this to be possible, the money we use must be incorruptible and not controlled by any person, group, organization, or government.

Bitcoin, often referred to as "freedom money," is a decentralized digital currency that operates outside the control of governments and financial institutions. It allows individuals to transact freely and securely without the need for intermediaries or third parties. Furthermore, it is fully transparent, and its ledger is public for anyone to see. In a world where governments routinely manipulate currencies and censor financial transactions, Bitcoin offers hope — a means of reclaiming our financial sovereignty and asserting our right to economic freedom.

It embodies the principles of liberty and self-determination that our founding fathers held dear. It is a reminder that true freedom cannot be bestowed upon us by benevolent rulers but must be proclaimed and defended by the people themselves. As you embark on your journey through life, I urge you to cherish the freedoms that we enjoy and to never take them for granted. Remember that freedom is not just a privilege; it is a responsibility. The responsibility to uphold the values of liberty, justice, and equal opportunity for yourself and future generations to come.

With all my love and blessings,

Your devoted father

NOTES FROM DAD

Tim Ruyle is a devoted husband to Sherry and a father of three. He cherishes the principles of family, faith, and innovation. With a background in mechanical engineering, Tim's professionalism is matched only by his commitment to his family and faith.

A family-oriented individual, Tim cherishes moments with his loved ones, prioritizing family vacations and gatherings, as well as enjoying shared interests such as Cardinals baseball, golf, and listening to classic '80s rock music.

In his manufacturing career of more than 32 years, Tim demonstrates a dedication to problem-solving and creativity, leveraging his mechanical engineering background and more than two decades of leadership experience.

Driven by his Catholic faith, Tim is an advocate for the sanctity of life, individual sovereignty, and personal freedom.

Embracing the potential of technological advancement, Tim finds intrigue in Bitcoin mining, exploring the opportunity for human flourishing presented by its unique properties.

In summary, Tim's life is a fusion of faith, family values, and curiosity-driven exploration, inspiring everyone to live, learn, and teach every day with humility.

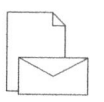

Tony Schneller

Dudes, Buddies, and Best Friends

To anyone reading this letter, I realize it is very personalized to my sons. If you are without a father or come from a fatherless home, I would encourage you to replace my sons' names with your own. If you are able, pretend that this letter is written to you. Let it speak to you. Let the Lord speak to you through it. If there is anything I can do for you, I would love the opportunity to connect with you, so do not hesitate to reach out.

Dear Brenden and Masen,

I love you. As your father, I wish I could say I would do anything to protect you, but I have failed. I have not protected you from the evils of this world to the extent I should have. I have set numerous bad examples as your dad, and I am so sorry. I allowed us to listen to bad music, watch bad movies, hang out regularly with people who have fallen into Satan's traps, lose my temper, say mean things, and so many other things that God should strike me dead for. I fail my family and my Heavenly Father on a daily basis, and I am ashamed.

But guys, thanks be to Jesus for saving me, and saving you, and for saving Mommy from our sins! I want to remind you that we were created by our Heavenly Father to bring Him glory and happiness. He loves you! Imagine how much you love our doggy Skyler, love Mommy, love Mamaw, love me, etc. He loves you infinitely more than that! It's impossible to fully comprehend! But I am so proud of you guys for placing your faith in Him and even taking the next step of being baptized! He saved you from hell through your faith by His incredibly loving grace! He's so proud of you, and so am I.

You're both such good dudes. It's really hard to explain how much I love you and how proud of you I am. The days each of you were born, I cried like crazy. I couldn't stop crying. I loved you so much before you were even born, but it really sunk in when I saw you for the first time. You were incredible! You were perfect, beautiful, amazing miracles God blessed Mommy and me with. I hope someday you get to experience that moment with your wife. You'll feel a warmth and loving feeling unlike you've ever felt before.

As I have been so fortunate to watch you guys grow into young men, my love for you grows, and I become even more proud of you, and more excited for your future that God has planned for you. It will be so amazing to watch your lives continue to develop. Not many young men have the resources and blessings that you do. I hope you take advantage of them and use them as much as you can to grow into the men God designed you to be. Along the way, remember that I will do everything I can to support you. Whether that be emotionally, mentally, spiritually, or financially, I will be here for you. Please do not forget that throughout your lives.

Some of the resources you have in front of you are only available to you by God's grace. He didn't have to let you be born into the wealthiest nation in the world. You could have been born in the slums of a third-world country. He didn't have to let you be intelligent and good-looking. You are, though! You're extremely handsome and so smart! He didn't have to let you be athletic. Instead, He blessed you with being very coordinated, strong, and agile. He didn't have to bless you with these things, so remember to be grateful because so many young men are not so fortunate.

Our family has been fortunate enough to send you to a great school, live in an affluent community, eat abundant and excellent food, and live in a comfortable home with great neighbors. Take advantage of these things as you can! Plug into the people at school and church! Learn about the things that interest you! Learn about God's love for you! Get a job doing something that you like and get paid for it! Then it won't seem like work! Start saving for things you want, like most of the world won't have a chance to do! If you start saving now, you won't have to borrow and fight for the rest of your life to get out of debt. I sure wish I would have started saving sooner. Our family's financial position would be so much stronger since we wouldn't have to be paying interest to banks on our loans. As Prov 22:7 says, "The rich rules over the poor, and the borrower is slave of the lender." Work to save money to buy your first car instead of borrowing from a bank, or relying on Mommy and me to buy it for you. This will teach you such a valuable life lesson of working hard and saving for what you want and set you on a track to financial independence.

You've both already accomplished so much at a young age! You're both showing a lot of qualities that strong leaders have. You care about and love people. You have strong personalities that exude confidence. You have intense opinions against evil things. You've grown your faith to the point that you know that you love Jesus and want to live your life as a Christian. You've discovered your interests. You've discovered the type of people you want to hang around. You've discovered places you love to visit. There's so much more for you to grow into, experience, learn, teach, enjoy, and love. There's also so much you'll discover that is wrong and broken about this world. Don't let that discourage you, though! These are all things that will help bring you closer to God if you let them.

Satan is going to try to knock you down. But stay plugged into your Lord and Savior. He will give you the strength, wisdom, knowledge, comfort, and peace to succeed in a world where many people and Satan will be against you. He will make you a warrior if you let Him. He will help you to make the right decisions, if you let Him. He will give you comfort when life gets hard if you let Him. He will show you the way out of hard situations if you let Him. You just have to stay connected to Him.

Talk to Him like He's your dad! Learn about Him through the Bible. Hang out with friends that love Him. Go to church as often as you can to worship Him and learn about Him. Listen for things within scripture and sermons that speak to you and that you can apply to your life in that moment. Remember the awesome things He's already done for you in your life. I get scared when I think about the evil things Satan is going to throw at you and me in our lives. But then I remember that God is on our side. He's not going to let Satan win. The Bible says Satan has already been defeated! So don't get discouraged when Satan's evil stuff gets you down. Be encouraged that it's an opportunity for your Heavenly Father to show you how powerful He is and how much He loves you. You already have such an advantage over the majority of the world in your faith alone. I've seen so many miracles in my life, and it just proves how much He really does watch over us because He loves us!

Make sure you enjoy making memories in doing things you enjoy. We've already done so many incredible things together, and I can't wait to do so many more! We've climbed mountains, snorkeled in the Caribbean, rode in fast cars and boats, flown in planes, eaten in some of the best restaurants in the world, and even brought other friends and family members with us! Let's keep having fun together and continue being best buddies and favorite dudes, and favorite buddies and best dudes! Two of the best memories I have with you guys is when we climbed the two different mountains together on our trip to Colorado in August of 2021. There were some tough parts of those climbs, but we kept pushing through, and it felt so good when we were done! We made it! What a feeling of accomplishment! And what a great way to spend time together.

Someday, I may not be around to be your father anymore, but I'll always be your Dad. I hope the day doesn't come anytime soon that I'm no longer on this earth. It could, though! We never know what the future holds. Just remember that I love you so much and that I am so proud of you. You guys are the best things that have ever happened to me. I wouldn't want to be the daddy of anyone else. You're the best gifts God has ever blessed me with. Brenden, You're my best buddy and my favorite dude. Masen, you're favorite buddy and my best dude.

Love,
Dad

NOTES FROM DAD

Tony Schneller was born and raised in St. Charles, MO, and lives there with his beautiful family. He and his wife have been married for 17 years, with two boys, ages 13 and 8. They love being outside, going on walks and hikes, boating, eating, and hanging out with friends. Tony grew up in a Christian home and had a very loving and supportive family. He has been a Christian for as long as he can remember. He was baptized about 10 years ago by his pastor, who he grew to be close friends with. He really started plugging more into God's Word within the last six years, through small men's groups and particularly a one-on-one program referred to as Operation Timothy. His participation has really helped him grow in my faith and develop his sense of purpose and direction as a Husband, Dad, Son, business owner, and leader.

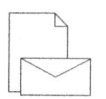

Afterword

Dad. Three simple letters, but a million's worth of significance of what that word means. It means you are a mentor, a teacher, a coach, a guidepost. Dads may not always realize it. It might get forgotten at times, but the role you play in your children's lives cannot be overstated. They look up to you, lean on you, love you.

This book offers a deep look at the role Dads play in our children's lives. It features more than 30 first-person stories of what fatherhood means to them. The stories range in tone—insightful, funny, thoughtful, emotional—but each has a common theme: that these men love being Dads and will do anything to be there for their children.

Working on this project has been unbelievable beyond words. I have had conversations with all the authors, traded emails, and shared intimate thoughts about what it means to be called Dad. I connected with someone whom I now consider a friend. We have vowed to stay in touch even as this project concludes. All because of the power of fatherhood.

We hope you have found inspiration from these personal stories, written by outstanding men who want to make their family — heck, the world — better.

It has been an honor to hear their stories.

Now, go do great things.

— Kyle Veltrop

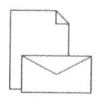

Jason Meinershagen

Conclusion

"The stories we tell ourselves shape our lives. They shape who we believe we are, and this belief translates into who we become."
— **John Assaraf**

If you read the entire book, thank you. Or maybe, like my mom, you skipped to the end to see how we wrapped it all up before you read the book. Either way, you're here, so thank you.

When I set out to compile this book, I always wanted to include an opportunity for dads to write their own note, but I only had some vague and rudimentary thoughts on how to present that challenge. Nearly a year into this project, and with only a month before final deadlines, I was blessed with the opportunity to attend a *"Legacy Letter Workshop"* hosted by Blake Brewer, the creator of the *"Legacy Letter Challenge."* I walked away from that experience with a better understanding of how to write my legacy letter and how to help you do likewise.

I **strongly** encourage you to visit https://www.legacyletter.com/ to learn more about the *"Legacy Letter Challenge"* directly from Blake. He's doing some amazing work in the arena of equipping dads with the knowledge and tools to leave a legacy for their children. I met with Blake after his workshop and am blessed to have him partner with us in this book by allowing us to share a summation of the notes I took from his *"Legacy Letter Workshop."*

If you're reading this book and are not a dad, that's okay. You have a story to tell and wisdom to share. Write this to someone you love; it doesn't have to be a child. Maybe you could write to your future self… all the things you want yourself to remember about this time in your life when you're older. Maybe you could write it to your past self. Wow, what an overwhelming thought! If I could go back in time and speak to my younger self, what advice would I give that young man in the mirror?! Whew!!! Oftentimes, writing to my younger self gives me a broader perspective and allows me to reflect on what's important in life…. It helps me keep my priorities in order. And it can be a cathartic and healing process when we write to ourselves.

My notes from the *"Legacy Letter Workshop"*

Why write a Legacy Letter?

1. It delivers hope by cutting through the noise.
2. It builds confidence by winning the heart.
3. It is "return-to-able"…they can go back to it over and over again.

Tips:

1. Be authentic. Share your feelings.
2. Write the way you talk.
3. Longer is not necessarily better.
4. We are not aiming for perfect. We're aiming for a finished letter.
5. Set a completion date.
6. Break it into the following sections:

Conclusion

Introduction Section:
- Set the stage for what's about to come.
- Answer the question, "*Why are you writing this letter?*"
- Consider providing context (i.e. the date when you write it.)

Apology Section:
- We're not perfect. We've said or done things that have hurt them, even if we didn't realize it. Apologies break down walls and set a tone of humility so they can receive the things you're about to say.
- Take responsibility. You were the adult, not them…even if you were young when you became a father.
- Express regret.
- Be sincere by expressing that you understand.
- Own up to your part, not theirs.
- Let go of the results. We cannot control their response.
- **DO NOT COME ACROSS AS THE VICTIM.**
    - If you do, whatever you write next will be lost.

I Love You Section:
- Answer the question that they're constantly asking in their heart, "*How do you really feel about me? How much do you love me?*"
- What is the potential lie your child could be telling themselves? (i.e. "*My dad will stop loving me if…*").
- What would change your love for them? Ideally, that'd be "*nothing*." So tell them that.
- What do they know I love? Consider comparing your love for them to something else they know you love (like maybe your favorite sports team).

I'm Proud of You Section:
- We don't want them wondering what makes us proud. We have to tell them.
- Focus on their character...who they are as a person...not what they've done or will ever do.
- What we affirm is what they'll repeat.

I Believe In You Section:
- Answer the question, *"Do you believe in me?"*
- When they're not achieving all they are capable of, we'll never shame them into achieving more. But we can affirm them in who they are and their abilities in a way that drives them to accelerate. Call them into who they can be.

Memories Section:
- Share a few of your favorite memories with them that show your love and pride for them, that you believe in them, that you like them, or to reframe a negative story that they're telling themselves.
- Every memory added to your letter is a bonus point that adds connection (see the quote at the beginning of this chapter.).

Advice Section:
- Share 3-5 pieces of advice.
- What do they need to hear from me?
- What do I want them to know as they move through this life?
- They don't care how much we know until they know how much we care.
- Consider framing it as advice to yourself, *"This is what I would share with myself 20 years ago."*
  - What is the advice?

- How did you come up with the advice?
- How would your life be different if you followed this advice?
- Use a tone of humility. "*I haven't always done the best at living out this advice, but my life has been better when I have.*"

Closing Paragraph:
- Answer the question, "*What are your hopes for the relationship going forward?*"
- Consider sharing your experience writing the letter for them. (i.e., "*I was filled with joy while writing this letter.*").
- The last line is your "legacy line." It's one line you want them to repeat over and over to themselves.

You're at a crossroads now. A point in your life when you can turn back and live as though nothing has changed, or you can turn the page and write the next chapter. We each have, within us, a story to tell. My story is mine to share, and your story is yours to share. Only *you* have lived the life you're living. You can either write the legacy you want to leave or let others write it when you're dead and gone. It's kind of like writing your own obituary...except way cooler because you have the opportunity to pour into your children in a way that will impact and shape who they become. And in a way that they can come back to time and time again.

Hopefully, you've been encouraged by the "Dadvice" you've read from all of us here and have been equipped with the tools to write your own note. Maybe you're like many of the dads who contributed to this book. Many of us will give this book to our children simply because we've contributed to it. We're confident they'll keep it because we've taken the time to write to them within its pages. But in the process of them having it because we're in it, they may read something another dad wrote that encourages them or equips them with a nugget of advice that they may need at any given moment. If you've read something in these pages that inspired or encouraged you, it's quite possible your children will one day also be inspired and encouraged by something they read here. Are they more likely to keep this book (and have that advice available to them) if you've written something personal to them in the following pages? I would emphatically say, yes. Yes, they would.

In the following pages, we've provided space for you to write your own chapter. You can either write your own story or let others write it for you. Which would you prefer? The legacy you leave for your children is for you to write. Get after it.

You got this!

I'm already praying God's words would flow through you onto the following pages, and that your note would impact those whom He wants it to impact. I'm also praying that your words would impact *you*!! Because there is a cathartic process of healing and restoration that takes place when we write. And in that journey of healing, we are drawn closer to God…to ourselves…and to our children.

And with that, I end…stop reading what others have to say about your place in this world and write your own story! Leave your own legacy. You're worth it!

Have a blessed day! Go **BE** the blessing!

For more information about "Legacy Letter Challenge" and "Legacy Letter Workshop" please visit: https://www.legacyletter.com/

NOTES

NOTES

NOTES

NOTES

NOTES

Made in the USA
Monee, IL
01 June 2024